DAILY HOMILIES

Ordinary Time — Year II

DAILY HOMILIES
Ordinary Time — Year II

DAILY HOMILIES
Ordinary Time — Year II

by

Rev. S. Joseph Krempa

In Three Volumes

Volume 1 Ordinary Time — Year 1
Volume 2 Ordinary Time — Year 2
Volume 3 Seasonal and Sanctoral

ALBA · HOUSE   NEW · YORK

SOCIETY OF ST. PAUL, 2187 VICTORY BLVD., STATEN ISLAND, NEW YORK 10314

Library of Congress Cataloging in Publication Data

Krempa, S. Joseph.
  Daily homilies.

    Contents: v. 1. Ordinary Time—year I;
v. 2. Ordinary Time—year II;
v. 3. Seasonal and sanctoral, Advent, Christmas,
Lent & Easter, and all obligatory memorials.
    1. Catholic Church—Sermons. 2. Sermons, American.
3. Christian saints—Biography. I. Title.
BX1756.K782D34   1984   252'.6   84-24224
ISBN 0-8189-0480-1 (vol. I)
ISBN 0-8189-0481-X (vol. II)
ISBN 0-8189-0479-8 (vol. III)
ISBN 0-8189-0483-6 (set)

Nihil Obstat:
Rev. Thomas E. Crane

Imprimatur:
Most Rev. Edward D. Head
Bishop of Buffalo
November 13, 1984

Designed, printed and bound in the United States of
America by the Fathers and Brothers of the
Society of St. Paul, 2187 Victory Boulevard,
Staten Island, New York 10314, as part of their
communications apostolate.

  2 3 4 5 6 7 8 9 (Current Printing: first digit).

PREFACE

During the week, a Mass celebrant encounters three groups of people: those who come daily, others who attend regularly and some who participate occasionally. A homilist has an obligation to each of these groups. One writer has compared it to preaching to a parade. Each day's scriptural selection is presented here with an exegetical and theological integrity of its own. Thematic unity for daily participants is balanced, however, by regular summaries so that the needs of the occasional participant are not disregarded.

The liturgical sense—the spiritual message as proclaimed —dominates these homilies although their deep background is based on technical analysis. A five minute reflection cannot be an occasion for a proper discussion of chiastic structure, Lukan sutures and the various levels of biblical criticism for people whose interests are more immediate and personal. Excellent and useful treatments of scriptural literary analysis abound, thankfully.

At the conclusion of this lengthy work, some important acknowledgments are necessary. I would like to thank Archbishop Thomas Kelly of Louisville, Kentucky for his inspiration and example; Rev. Vincent Donovan of Laurel, Maryland for his discursive, but always insightful, Monday morning conversations; the Woodstock Theological Center Library at Georgetown University in Washington, D.C. for the generous permission to use their collection; special thanks to the community at the daily evening Mass at St. Nicholas Church in Laurel, Maryland whose patience, faith and encouragement made this book possible.

A distinct word of gratitude to my Ordinary, Bishop Edward Head of Buffalo, New York for his kindness. He is a man of extraordinary common sense who, over the past decade, has healed a diocese. Through his deep trust in everything Catholic, he has made Western New York a home for a wide, lively and diverse Catholic family.

Rev. S. Joseph Krempa

to Rev. Eugene Weber,
priest of West Virginia,
magnificent pastor,
sure guide on the Christian journey,
who brings the Word to life every day

MONDAY — First Week of the Year

Mk 1:14-20

First Reading

The First Book of Samuel is an anecdotal history and part of the theological story of the passage of the Israelites from the era of the Judges to the beginnings of the monarchy. The figure who sheds this transition is Samuel, whose family background is portrayed in today's first reading. This moving story of the love shown by Elkanah and his barren wife, Hannah, is the backdrop to a profound turning point in Israel's political and religious experience. The setting is the traditional shrine at Shiloh, home of the tribal league, where Hannah was one of many annual pilgrims. Soon, she will give birth to a son under whom the entire system will dissolve into a new era of kings and prophets. Beneath the surface of ordinary things, great events are brewing.

Gospel Reading

Great events are brewing in today's Gospel reading. We join in Mark's Gospel at the beginning of Jesus' public ministry. The kingdom announced by John has come to life in Jesus. It starts with the call of His first disciples: Andrew, Simon, James and John. They abandon their trades and leave their families to follow this traveling rabbi. Their response to Christ is so thorough that it becomes a model for all future kinds of discipleship.

What binds disciples throughout the world together is the effort to deal seriously with Jesus as Lord of their life. To remain with family and job as a Christian disciple requires many subtle

MONDAY — First Week of the Year
1 S 1:1-8   *Mk 1:14-20*

First Reading

The First Book of Samuel is an anecdotal history and part of the theological story of the passage of the Israelites from the era of the Judges to the beginnings of the monarchy. The figure who shepherds this transition is Samuel whose family background is portrayed in today's first reading. This moving story of the love shared by Elkanah and his barren wife, Hannah, is the backdrop for a profound turning point in Israel's political and religious experience. The setting is the traditional shrine at Shiloh, home of the tribal league, where Hannah was one of many annual pilgrims. Soon, she will give birth to a son under whom this entire system will dissolve into a new era of kings and prophets. Beneath the surface of ordinary things, great events are brewing.

Gospel Reading

Great events are brewing in today's Gospel reading. We join Mark's Gospel at the beginning of Jesus' public ministry. The kingdom announced by John has come to life in Jesus. It starts with the call of His first disciples: Andrew, Simon, James and John. They abandon their trades and leave their families to follow this traveling rabbi. Their response to Christ is so thorough that it becomes a model for all future kinds of discipleship.

What binds disciples throughout the world together is the effort to deal seriously with Jesus as Lord of their life. To remain with family and job as a Christian disciple requires many subtle judgments but can be as challenging, radical and rewarding as is leaving everything behind to follow the Lord.

Point

Underneath the apparent routine of things, profound forces are at work.

TUESDAY — First Week of the Year
1 S 1:9-20   Mk 1:21-28

First Reading

The prophet Samuel was the executive, legislative and judicial branches of government all wrapped up in one. He was a circuit-riding prosecutor, jury, judge, military commander and religious leader who oversaw the movement from Israel's existence as a loose family of tribes into a nation united under a king. Because of Samuel's pivotal importance, the memory of his birth acquired almost mythic status.

The first reading is the poignant story of Hannah and the ridicule she endured from her fruitful co-wife Peninah. As Hannah pours her heart out in prayer, she is reprimanded by Eli, who represents the twilight of the old Elianic priesthood. The irony loaded into this scene is that the priesthood and social order Eli symbolizes is on the edge of extinction as the child Hannah conceives ushers in a new era. This story shows that Samuel was a decisive figure not by accident or luck but because God had selected him from his very beginnings. In the same way, each of us has not only a general vocation to the married, single or religious life; we have as well a specific place in God's design, the dimensions of which might not be entirely clear to us at present.

Gospel Reading

An exorcism is the first sign of Jesus' power in Mark's Gospel. There are all kinds of spirits from which the Lord releases us. We are liberated not simply from the devil but from greed, hate, jealousy and despair so that we can see with greater clarity the purpose God has for us beyond the various goals we set for ourselves. Frequently, the two purposes diverge. It takes effort and grace to have them converge so that our will and God's will are synchronous.

Point

The heart of Christian peace is the ability to say, as did the Lord, "Thy will be done."

WEDNESDAY — First Week of the Year
1 S 3:1-10, 19-20   Mk 1:29-39

First Reading

"In those days," says the first reading, "revelation was uncommon and vision infrequent." Ordinarily, Eli's sons would have inherited his priesthood. But they disqualified themselves by their sexual and sacrilegious escapades at the Shiloh shrine. Samuel was dedicated to God's service by his mother and represents a new thrust in God's plan for Israel. It was a new direction that would emerge from within the tradition. Samuel was unable to recognize the voice of God until Eli had taught him how to discern what is from God.

Voices in the night or within ourselves do not carry labels. Like Samuel, we learn to discern experiences in the light of our tradition. We do not start from scratch in trying to understand the meaning of love, birth, death and life. Twenty centuries of

Christian experience and teaching help us interpret those very personal movements of the Spirit within us.

Gospel Reading

The secret of discerning the Holy Spirit is found in today's Gospel reading. After some healings, Jesus goes to a lonely place in the desert to be absorbed in prayer. The key to discerning the voice of God is prayer—not busy, recitative prayer but silent communion. We learn to recognize the voice of God much as a mother can pick out her baby's sounds from a noisy crowd or as a musician can hear melody lines missed by the non-specialist. It is no surprise that revelation was uncommon and vision infrequent in the days of Eli's sons. They were too busy to look and listen.

Point

The depths of prayer are not reserved for a spiritual elite. They are for everyone who, like Samuel, will learn to recognize the call of God.

THURSDAY — First Week of the Year
1 S 4:1-11   *Mk 1:40-45*

First Reading

This is not the way biblical battles are supposed to turn out, especially after the Israelites wheel out the ark of the covenant to protect them. They lost this battle with the Philistines. Perhaps they saw the ark as a lucky charm that insured God's automatic protection even though their own fidelity to the covenant was gone. Eli's sons were probably typical of the majority of Israelites in that regard. They saw the ark as a "rabbit's foot" that would work irrespective of their faith or lack of it. The Philistines captured the ark and placed it inside their temple. It did not turn out to be a great prize, however. Their idols broke apart and the entire city was afflicted with hemorrhoids. As the ark was rapidly moved to a second and third city, the hemorrhoids went with it. Finally the Philistines paid the Israelites to take back the ark. The lesson of this strange story is that God is in charge of events but will not be manipulated as an amulet.

Gospel Reading

A magical God is also at issue in today's Gospel reading. Jesus cures a leper who, in those days, was segregated as a special object of divine disfavor. After healing him, Jesus warns him not to report this incident to anyone. This feature of Jesus' ministry is special to Mark's Gospel. Possibly, the Lord knew that people would place a political, economic or magical gloss on His Messiahship as news of His healings became known. It is only in the central chapter of Mark's Gospel that Jesus reveals to the disciples that He is a Messiah who must suffer and then die.

Point

Faith is not magic. Our relationship with the Lord should not be a commercial one. We can test whether we see Jesus as lucky charm or Master. If the way we think, feel and live begins to center around Him, that is discipleship.

FRIDAY — First Week of the Year
1 S 8:4-7, 10-22   Mk 2:1-12

First Reading

The First and Second Books of Samuel collect a number of old Israelite traditions. Some are pro-monarchy while others are violently anti-royalist. Today's first reading comes from a tradition suspicious of kings and kingship. The assaults of the encroaching Philistines continue to exhaust the Israelites. Various tribal leaders approach Samuel to indicate their need of a central political force to unify them against the common enemy. Until now, they were loosely linked by clan and faith without any strong institutions to unite them. Samuel responds with a description of the dark underside of kingship: search and seizure, taxes, the draft, servitude and a government saddled tightly on everyone's back. Given a king, they will turn from God as their life is gradually defined not by the covenant but by ambition and political advantage. The leaders still press for a king. Finally, Samuel is instructed to ratify their request and anoint a king. This is a major institutional shift in Israel's life as Israel becomes like other nations in more ways than this one.

Choices we make have consequences with which we must live. God remains with us even when we choose badly, just as He remained with Israel through good kings and bad through the prophets.

Gospel Reading

A paralyzed man is lowered through a roof into the presence of Jesus. After a series of cures, exorcisms and healings, Jesus looks at this particular individual and, for the first time in Mark's Gospel, says something unprecedented: "Your *sins* are forgiven!" Perhaps Jesus saw that the man's real problem was a heart paralyzed with guilt. His pronouncement incensed the Pharisees who were stunned by such a claim of divine power. Then, He tells the man to walk home to prove that he had been healed. Often, a spiritual dysfunction compounds our daily problems. Spiritual disharmony might not cause our problems but it certainly blocks our attempts to find solutions. There is no airtight separation between the spiritual and practical sides of our life.

Point

It is common to say, "When everything gets straightened out in my life, then I'll get right with God." The reverse is true. When we get right with God, things in our life begin to rectify.

SATURDAY — First Week of the Year
1 S 9:1-4, 17-19; 10:1   Mk 2:13-17

First Reading

We have the stories of God's call to two people in today's readings. The first call is to Saul as Israel's first king. Saul looked like a king—straight out of central casting. He was tall, dark and handsome. While searching for some of his father's lost flock, he chances across Samuel. Samuel chose him possibly because they were from the same tribe or because the tribe of Benjamin was the smallest and the others would not feel threatened by a Benjaminite king. Saul is anointed privately. Much more would be required of him than an impressive appearance. During the coming week, we will see a little of the life and career of Saul.

Gospel Reading

We have the call of Levi the tax collector, who tradition identifies with Matthew. The tax collector was a person especially abhorrent to the Jews and perhaps to all cultures. Jesus intensifies the leaders' suspicion by dining with a whole gaggle of tax collectors. This scene reminds us that our eucharistic celebration should be a moment when people can feel free to be "off-stage" for a while, leave their swords at the door and simply be brothers and sisters in the Lord.

We might contrast Saul and Levi. In Saul's case, there will be degeneration. Levi remained faithful. The contrast shows that follow-through is as important as the initial moment of decision. That first moment might be an ordination, marriage or any decisive point in our life. How we implement and incorporate that decision into our life on a routine basis is as important as the drama of that first response to the Lord.

Point

The follow-through and conclusion of our Christian life are as momentous as its beginning.

MONDAY — Second Week of the Year
1 S 15:16-23   *Mk 2:18-22*

First Reading

This week, we will witness a tragedy in the story of Saul. The reign of Israel's first king began bright with promise and ended in the shadows of witchcraft, insanity and suicide. This episode gives us some insight into the reason for Saul's decline.

To repay an ancient grudge, the prophet Samuel declared a holy war against the Amalekites. The holy war was a primitive interpretation of justice which was thought to demand the extermination of a non-Israelite enemy in a grim holocaust to God. Saul allowed his troops to retain some livestock for their own private sacrifice and he also spared the life of the Amalekite king. This enraged Samuel. In this admittedly humane gesture of Saul, we can see a seed of failure. He acceded to the desires of his troops and arranged sacrifices without the approval of the religious leader Samuel, thereby blurring the lines between religion and politics. That is why Samuel declares obedience to the prophetic word to be more important than sacrifices. He then withdraws his support from Saul's monarchy, effectively excommunicating him. A message for us from this reading is that religious rituals have value as prayer when they express a fundamental obedience to God.

Gospel Reading

Today's Gospel reading is about fasting. Mark uses this incident to explain to his Roman Christian audience why the early Church restored the practice of fasting which Jesus and His disciples had abandoned. The traditional purpose of fasting was to repair the effects of sin and to bridge the gap between people and God. Jesus states that no such distance exists while He is among us. When He returns to the Father, the time to resume fasting will begin. Even when the Church incorporated many Old Testament practices, it was new wine in the old wineskins and new cloth on the old cloak. Temples, fasting, sacrificial language, Sabbath and priesthood were not seen by the early Church as bridges over an Old Testament gap to a distant God. Rather, they celebrated the presence of the Spirit of the Risen Lord among us.

Point

Our religious practices do not seek to reach out to a remote God but to focus the Lord's presence among us.

TUESDAY — Second Week of the Year
1 S 16:1-13   *Mk 2:23-28*

First Reading

Once again, Samuel anoints a young man as king to give him the spirit of God and prophetic approval. This romantic description of David's selection implies that Saul's dynasty is stillborn. This private anointing of David is only a beginning.

David refuses to take Samuel's anticipatory liturgical hint to lead a rebellion against Saul. Instead he will slowly fulfill the promise by gradually and legitimately advancing toward the kingship. Then he will be anointed again as he is acclaimed and accepted by the people. David cooperates with the spirit he has received and rises in power. Saul smothers that spirit as his power and authority ebb away. It is important not only to receive the Spirit but to remain in contact with that gift.

Gospel Reading

We remain in contact with the Spirit through the sacraments and our religious practices. It is possible for a mechanical application of rules to detract from our spiritual life. This Gospel reading is one of a series of controversies between Jesus and the religious leaders. Yesterday's reading dealt with fasting. This reading concerns the Sabbath because the early Church had switched its weekly observance from the Sabbath to Sunday. The Lord tells us that when religious observances become ends in themselves rather than vehicles for communion with God, they can become roadblocks. It is possible to obey rules simply because a person loves rules rather than God. The Sabbath was originally intended to celebrate the covenant and liberation. The religious establishment had turned it into a burden and a penance. We can become slaves of practices if they fail to free us for communication with the Father.

Point

The Spirit is a gift that we must bring to fulfillment in our lives. That fulfillment comes through frequent contact with the Spirit.

WEDNESDAY — Second Week of the Year
1 S 17:32-33, 37, 40-51   *Mk 3:1-6*

First Reading

The story of David and Goliath is the more ennobling of the two most famous stories about David. It provides a pattern around which hundreds of tales have been built to comfort dragonkillers and whistleblowers. It is the classic confrontation of the lean, young shepherd boy against the armored giant. The real contrast in the story, however, is between David's electric courage and Saul's paralyzing fear of the Philistines. David provides the spark for victory while Saul sits to the side terrified and impotent.

This scene was built upon an Israelite victory over the Philistines in which David had a part. As the story was told and retold, David became younger, Goliath became bigger and the other participants gradually dropped away. Still, it remains a story of the power of God working through an individual to give fresh vigor to a stagnant situation.

Gospel Reading

Jesus "works" on the Sabbath by healing a man with a withered hand. As the Pharisees wonder why such a cure could not be delayed to the next day, Jesus responds by speaking of the urgency of the kingdom. To delay and wait for the right moment might be to settle for stalemate. In fact, to leave the hand withered would be complicity in evil. The cures of Jesus in Mark's Gospel comprise more than a series of good deeds. Jesus is confronting the powers of darkness either directly or in their effects. We seldom confront the devil directly, exorcist-style. What we meet are the effects of evil found in social, economic or personal dislocation. We encounter the tensions and hurts caused by evil.

Point

In helping others, we are projecting the kingdom. The residue of evil might seem to be a massive Goliath. The good we do appears like David's stone. We never know the full effect of the pieces of love and forgiveness that we let loose into the world.

THURSDAY — Second Week of the Year
1 S 18:6-9; 19:1-7   *Mk 3:7-12*

First Reading

David's rise to the kingship had been so glamorized over the years that it became epic and legendary. We might examine some aspects of his character that assisted his success. He was a shrewd judge of people, masterful at political timing and very much a strategic thinker. Secondly, from the tiny lyric in to-day's first reading about his killing ten thousands, it seems that he did a great deal more than kill Goliath. He was, some scholars believe, somewhat of a Robin Hood with his own private army engaged in a roving guerilla war. Thirdly, he was charismatic enough to attract the affection of Saul's daughter and son as well as the jealousy of Saul. Despite the upbeat ending of today's reading, there was no real reconciliation between David and Saul. As David's star rises, we will see the eclipse of Saul's glory and sanity. Obsessive jealousy will consume Saul, swaying his judgment as king and his prowess as warrior. Jealousy is the emotional shorthand we use for the deeper currents of hate that flooded Saul's heart.

Gospel Reading

Jealousy also appears in today's Gospel reading. Mark

shows Jesus' popularity as a healer. He silences the demons who recognize Him as Son of God. It will be necessary in Mark's story that Jesus suffer first to show the connection between suffering and glory. It is only on Calvary that a Gentile centurion will admit that truly this was a Son of God. Here, Mark pictures all the people of Israel, except the leaders, gathered around Jesus. Because of their envy, the leaders fail to see what is obvious to the people. Their jealousy is emotional shorthand for the decision of unbelief which they had made deep within themselves. There are a variety of emotional masquerades for unbelief.

Point

The floor on which our spiritual life is built should not simply be emotion. It is a decision either of faith or unbelief.

FRIDAY — Second Week of the Year
1 S 24:3-21   *Mk 3:13-19*

First Reading

The reconciliation between David and Saul in yesterday's reading was only temporary. Here, we have Saul expending his time and resources hunting for David despite his own continuing conflict with the Philistines. This scene captures a moment of truth. Saul is in a highly vulnerable position. David refuses to take advantage of him and simply cuts a corner of Saul's cloak to prove that he does not seek to assassinate him. In this single gesture, Saul realizes the inevitability of David's kingship. It was perhaps Saul's last lucid moment. The clouds of his hate and envy parted briefly and he realized that God's will for Israel's future lay in David and not in himself. It is an important moment of majesty and pity.

Gospel Reading

Jesus goes to the mountain. The mountain is the biblical clue of an impending moment of great importance. Up to this point, we have seen Jesus' healings and controversies. Now, He selects out the Twelve from the crowd of disciples. These Twelve have seen the power of Jesus as well as the power of His opposition. Jesus did not leave the written New Testament behind as His legacy. Rather, He left the Twelve as the carriers of His message and ministry. Jesus will now begin to teach these Twelve more intimately about the kingdom and about God, forgiveness and judgment.

We too know the power of Jesus as well as the power of His opponents; we too are carriers not only of the tradition about Jesus but also of His work; we too should be more aware of the ways of the Triune God than is the rest of mankind.

Point

Just as David and the Apostles, with all their shortcomings, were vehicles for the fulfillment of God's purposes, so we are fragile instruments of Jesus' ministry to those around us.

SATURDAY — Second Week of the Year
2 S 1:1-4, 11-12, 19, 23-27   *Mk 3:20-21*

First Reading

Saul is dead. David chants a lament which recalls and extolls Saul and Jonathan in their best moments. Saul's career began when he was anointed by Samuel at the height of his powers. Filled with the rushing spirit as the oil glistened on his forehead, he was a brand new king bursting with promise for an emerging nation. At the end, exhausted by the Philistine war he could not win, deserted by his advisors, driven by the blackest

emotions, groping for solace from witches and ghosts, surrounded by the enemy on Mount Gilboa, Saul commits
suicide. The Philistines then nailed his body to their city wall.
Saul's monarchy and the Word of God as expressed in the
traditional prophetic religion had taken separate paths. Samuel
withdrew his support; David skillfully created his own popular
power base. Saul was left alone, destined to be only a transi-
tional leader between the twilight of one era and the dawn of
another. He would leave behind no male heirs and later tradition will almost completely ignore him. Yet, he laid the foundations on which David will build the kingdom of Israel.

Gospel Reading

Jesus' neighbors and family fail to understand Him. Mark
uses this to emphasize that the bonds of the new community
Jesus creates are not based on ethnicity or blood but on faith.
The early Church was not centered in Nazareth or Galilee. It
was very much a community grounded on faith and the experience of the risen Lord. This is also the bond of the Church
today.

Point

*Jesus created a community and not a collection of inde-
pendent hermits. We should try to share the joys and sufferings
of our discipleship with each other.*

MONDAY — Third Week of the Year
2 S 5:1-7, 10   Mk 3:22-30

First Reading

David finally comes to his own. After years in the trenches
with his people, he is acclaimed a great military hero and

anointed at the traditional shrine at Hebron. The split between
the tribes of the north and south that dominated Saul's reign is
healed as both regions choose him as king. His first act is to
capture Jerusalem as his capital city. Until now, there has been
no central capital. Israel was much like the fifty states without a
Washington, D.C. David selected Jerusalem because it was
neutral territory. It became known as the City of David. David's
second step was to defeat the Philistines once and for all. We
have a new king and a new era which will be recalled for
centuries as the glory days for Israel. The military and political
victories of David will become the metaphors for what Jesus
will do in the spiritual domain. The Messiah will be described
not primarily as a new Moses or a new prophet but as a king
patterned after David.

Gospel Reading

The Jewish leaders realized that Jesus possessed extraordinary supernatural power. They claimed that it was diabolic.
Jesus makes a three-pronged response. He points to the effects
of His ministry: healings and forgiveness are the very opposite
of Satanic work. Secondly, He says that a strong man's house
can be raided only if the owner is first bound up. A single
instance of healing and forgiveness shows that the rule of evil is
not inviolate and can be ruptured. We do not have to settle for
living under the domination of evil. Finally, Jesus indicates that
to so distort reality—to say that the obvious works of God are
evil—is a blasphemy against whatever inborn capacity we
have for distinguishing good from evil. It is a sin against the
Holy Spirit because such a person has shut out whatever light
could prove to be his salvation. This was the early Church's
explanation for the Jewish leaders' opposition to Jesus.

Point

David realized that God gave him victory because he saw

His presence in the events of his life. To confine the Spirit to certain restricted paths is a sin against that Spirit.

TUESDAY — Third Week of the Year
2 S 6:12-15, 17-19   Mk 3:31-35

First Reading

David dances before the ark which he brought up to Jerusalem. There is more here than an act of devotion or ritual abandon. By bringing the ark to Jerusalem, David rescued this ancient symbol of the covenant from neglect and tied together the separate religious and political sectors of Israel in a single city—the very thing Saul was condemned for attempting. Until now, the ark generally rested at Shiloh but had been moved to different shrines among the tribes while suffering long periods of abandonment as well. When David brought it to Jerusalem, the city became the political and religious capital of North and South. The city gave visible expression to Israelite identity and to the spiritual bond of the covenant. Jerusalem would forever be the symbol of Jewish glory and suffering. It would be the focus of intense love, hate, faith, hope and prayer. We can see the vital psychological and cultural role Jerusalem played in the Israelite soul from the psalms that praise, glorify, extol and lament the city: "Jerusalem, built as a city with compact unity; to it the tribes go up, the tribes of the Lord!"

Gospel Reading

Jesus emphasizes the superiority of spiritual relationships to family ties. His followers would be united not by political or economic interests but by the desire to hear the Word of God and keep it. "To hear the Word of God and keep it" conjures images of heroic martyrs and saintly missionaries. There is also the difficult work of taking Jesus seriously in all the areas of our life. It is this common discipleship that links us here today more closely to each other than to many of our relatives. The symbol of our spiritual unity is not a city like Jerusalem but the celebration of the Eucharist which joins us to the universal Church. Through us, the world is brought into the Father's love and bonded again to Jesus.

Point

We are the point of contact between the Gospel and the world. This discipleship is our common bond.

WEDNESDAY — Third Week of the Year
2 S 7:4-17   *Mk 4:1-20*

First Reading

David had wanted to build a permanent structure for the ark as an annex of his palace. Nathan, representing the rapidly waning independence of the religious order, saw danger in such an overt politicization of the ark. In today's reading, David receives an oracle through the prophet Nathan in which God refuses to permit the construction of a temple. The tent housing the ark would remain, for now, a reminder of leaner days. After asserting sovereignty in David's career and kingship, God promises to dwell not in a stone temple but in the house and dynasty of David. These verses are the birthplace of the theology of the Messiah. The historical reference is to Solomon. The prophetic and inspired reference is to the true Son of David whose kingdom will last forever—Jesus. The deep promise of this oracle from Nathan is that God would not be localized and confined in a temple, but would be present in people, events and history.

Gospel Reading

Jesus tells the famous parable of the seed sown at random. This parable has several levels to it. It describes the ultimate ineffectiveness of those who oppose the Word of God which still falls onto some good soil to generate a magnificent harvest. It describes the differences among hearers of the Word— indifference and disregard are always part of the response to the Church's mission. It is a catalog of spiritual types, of parishioners everywhere. Its last point is that the Word will continue to be preached and that no era would be completely devoid of God's Word. Through this preached and sacramental Word, the Lord continues to be present in people, events and history.

Point

There is no chaining the Word of God. It still lives and grows among people according to the mystery of grace.

THURSDAY — Third Week of the Year
2 S 7:18-19, 24-29   *Mk 4:21-25*

First Reading

In gratitude for the divine promise through Nathan of an everlasting dynasty, David reflects on the point to which he and Israel have been elevated by God. The fate of both have become intertwined. In this prayer, David gives expression to the soul of his kingship at its best and most obedient. He acknowledges that everything he has received is a gift and asks that his line be a beneficial influence on all Israel. David has become more than a political leader. A special covenant with David is now overlaid on the Sinai covenant. The institution of kingship is here given a location in theology, ceremony and psalm. David's royal line is now seen as an instrument of salvation in some enigmatic and universal sense, as the cornerstone of a worldwide and everlasting kingdom. David's prayer will provide a vocabulary for the prophets and the early Church to describe the work of God in His Messiah—king, kingdom, domain, dynasty, eternal rule. God's promise to David would not be fulfilled politically but in the realm of the spirit.

Gospel Reading

This saying of Jesus about light is placed by each evangelist in a different context. Mark uses the Lord's words to explain the temporary concealment of the kingdom. The great covenant with David was fulfilled in Jesus. But the promised splendor and majesty were not given the political or economic form which Mark's audience seemed to expect. The Lord addresses the kingdom's invisibility. Although it will be made known at the end of time, its hiddenness does not mean that it is devoid of power. Amid the forces that seek to wreck human dignity and community, the forces of the kingdom are at work to heal and make whole. That they do not assemble in battle fatigues does not mean they are absent.

Point

The kingdom promised to David and fulfilled in Jesus is a spiritual one composed of human lives and loves, not a military empire. That makes it deathless.

FRIDAY — Third Week of the Year
2 S 11:1-10, 13-17   *Mk 4:26-34*

First Reading

In this first reading, we have the second most famous

episode from David's life—his tryst with Bathsheba, wife of Uriah. The dramatic details of this story must have quickly grown from an item of downstairs palace gossip into one of the great redeeming tales about David. Bathsheba became pregnant after sexual intercourse with David. He tried to entice her husband Uriah, home on leave, to spend time with her to provide a plausible cover for her pregnancy. Uriah refused to go to bed with his wife, saying that he would not do so until the war with the Ammonites was won. It may well be that Uriah knew exactly what was going on and refused to provide David with an easy excuse. David had Uriah killed in battle so that he could marry his wife. David's essential sin here was not lust but greed. His career had progressed so successfully that he began to try to play God and to disregard the covenant of Sinai. After all, he thought he had his own special covenantal protection from God. David's recognition that he had sinned in this episode will retrieve him from the brink of corruption. Although power corrupts, David will not go the way of Saul. It was David's capacity to repent that made him an attractive example in Israel's history.

Gospel Reading

We have two parables. Seed grows on its own as the sower waits; a tiny mustard seed grows into a large bush. The point of these images is that there is more at work in the spread of the kingdom than human effort. We cannot reduce the growth or decline of the Church to empirical factors alone. Jesus' ministry seemed to have many hindrances. He says to His disciples, "Relax! Just as the Father produces the harvest, so will He produce the kingdom."

The seed of faith is sown in all the baptized. We do not lose that baptismal Spirit even when we sin. We do not re-baptize those whose sins are forgiven. How an individual responds to that Spirit is the subject of the Last Judgment.

Point

The Spirit of our baptism is always with us. This is at once the majesty and tragedy of mankind.

SATURDAY — Third Week of the Year
2 S 12:1-7, 10-17   Mk 4:35-41

First Reading

Nathan, the court prophet, steps forward. He does not challenge David's sin with Bathsheba directly. He extracts the core of the offense and places it in a different context where David could view it with dispassion. He asks for David's judgment about a wealthy rancher who steals a poor man's lamb. David is enraged at such raw greed and demands retribution. In one of the most dramatic moments of the Old Testament, Nathan tells David, "You are that man!" He then pronounces God's judgment that David will be dishonored in broad daylight as Uriah was. David admits his guilt and is forgiven.

Still, what we would call the temporal punishment due to sin, the effect of his wrongdoing, remains. His pride and treachery will be imitated by his family and court. The sin with Bathsheba is not an isolated act but part of a larger milieu of David's own making for which he will eventually pay a price. This incident is the turning point of David's life.

Gospel Reading

The story of the storm on the lake is preserved in the Gospels as a source of encouragement for the early Christians and for us. Very early on, the storm was seen as representing difficulties of any kind in the Church. Persecution, ostracism, dishonesty and dissent were all "storms" that wracked the early Christian communities. This reading reminded them that the Lord was still with them. He would be a source of calm in the middle of the storm. Whether our storms are public or private, the message remains the same. Jesus is with us to bring peace and tranquility in the storm. Even in our failings, He is there to bring us back.

Point

Even when we sin, we are not left alone to find our way back. The Lord is there to guide us home.

MONDAY — Fourth Week of the Year
2 S 15:13-14, 30; 16:5-13   *Mk 5:1-20*

First Reading

David's affair with Bathsheba was a turning point in his life; after it, things seemed to fall apart. David had created an environment of deception and backstabbing that pervaded his family and court. Just as David had taken Uriah's wife, now David's son, Absalom, wanted to grab the throne. Absalom is not as corrupt as we might imagine him to be. His sister had been raped by her half-brother, David's oldest son. David did nothing about it for two years. Such inaction enraged Absalom, who finally revenged his sister by murdering the offending brother. He perceived David's delay as weakness and led a revolt to seize the throne. In today's first reading, David and his court leave Jerusalem. Along the way, he is met by a member of Saul's tribe who curses him in a hint of a larger unrest abroad in the land. These two events signal that the eternity promised David's line would be spiritual and not dynastic.

Gospel Reading

The story of the demons cast into the swine illustrates two

points both for the early Church as well as for ourselves. First, Jesus is in Gentile territory since Jews had no reason to raise pigs (unless these were extremely liberal Jews). The kingdom Jesus embodied would not be an intramural Jewish affair—its expanse was to be universal. Secondly, Mark is explaining why the preaching of the Gospel seemed to flourish years later in this "pagan" region of the Ten Cities. By expelling these demons, Jesus created an environment conducive to the preaching of the Word despite the initial hesitations of the townspeople.

We all create an environment. Our private spiritual life radiates to others. Some see this as the significance of the halo used in Christian iconography. Just as Jesus sends the healed man back to his own family, so we bring our spiritual resources to bear, often unknowingly, upon those we meet.

Point

Jesus works not only through our words and deeds, but also through what we are and what we have become.

TUESDAY — Fourth Week of the Year
2 S 18:9-10, 14, 24-25, 30-19:3   *Mk 5:21-43*

First Reading

Absalom is killed. His head was caught between tree branches and he was left hanging as his colt ran off. One of David's men came by and stabbed him to death. The first reading focuses on David's anguish. "Absalom, my son!" We see in this a duality in David's personality. Here, the slayer of the Philistines, Edomites, Ammonites and Moabites laments the death of his rebellious son. The image of David's grief contains a parable of God's love for us. Despite everything Absalom had done against him, he remained David's son. Even in our failures and occasional rebellions, God continues to love us.

Gospel Reading

The Gospel reading reveals how we might discover the Father's love. Mark sandwiches one miracle within another. The emphasis is less on the miracles than on the faith of the ailing woman and the girl's father. Mark's Gospel is usually very elliptical. The amount of detail in these episodes is extraordinary. Possibly, these stories served as case studies of faith. Each detail was a springboard for a significant catechetical point. Both people trusted the Lord. Jairus broke through the prejudices of his class and disregarded the danger to his reputation in approaching Jesus. The woman who exhausted her savings on doctors worked her way painfully through the crowd to touch Jesus. We all meet such boundary situations when we come to the end of our resources and are up against the wall. All the props on which we relied seem useless and we are forced to confront God. Such moments can disclose God to us in a new way. Like the man who lifts an automobile to save his trapped son, we can discover in boundary situations profound spiritual strength otherwise trapped inside us by the lack of challenge.

Point

A crisis enables us to break through our everyday religiosity to touch the healing power of God that always surrounds us.

WEDNESDAY — Fourth Week of the Year
2 S 24:2, 9-17   Mk 6:1-6

First Reading

In this first reading, we have the baffling episode of a census. David is confronted through the prophet Gad with a choice of one of three punishments for a census he had authorized: three years of famine, three months of flight or three days of pestilence. In any of the three, many of the people David had counted in the census would die. We can only speculate why the Bible reports such a judgment. It may have been because David treated the population as his own personal property and not as God's people entrusted to him. It might indicate that he was placing more confidence in the police power of the state than in the covenant to maintain national harmony. More probably, it was a prophetic condemnation of the growing power of the bureaucratic state. David was slowly shifting the people's allegiance from the covenant to the monarchy. He was creating an early form of civil religion in which religious institutions and the covenant became political tools.

Gospel Reading

Jesus is rejected by His own people. This apparently trivial episode had critical meaning for the early Church, which was deeply perplexed by the refusal of Jesus' own people to accept Him. This act of rejection sums up the basic issue of Jesus' entire ministry. The religious leaders saw Jesus as everything except what He said He was. They saw Jesus as just "one of the folks" who was for them a political problem. They saw nothing deeper than that.

Point

Faith and religion do not simply provide a religious vocabulary for otherwise secular phenomena. Faith puts us in contact with a dimension of reality that undergirds and supports everything we do. That is what the covenant did and what Jesus does.

THURSDAY — Fourth Week of the Year
1 K 2:1-4, 10-12   *Mk 6:7-13*

First Reading

David's dying instructions to one of his sons, Solomon, are an odd mixture. On the one hand, in today's reading, he charges Solomon and his successors to obey God and to follow the Law—a standard by which all later kings of Israel would be judged. On the other hand, in a section omitted from today's reading, David instructs Solomon to even up some old scores. He is to kill Joab, the slayer of Absalom and to punish Shimei, the member of Saul's tribe of Benjamin who had cursed David years before. David's death is marked by the ambiguity that colored his life and reign. His fidelity to the God of Israel and his moments of deep repentance were coupled with the startling brutality and wantonness of royal power. The throne now passes to Solomon who will inherit David's glory as well as his excesses.

Gospel Reading

This Gospel reading gives a scriptural basis for Christian missionary activity. Although the style described seems geared more to Gentile areas than to the villages of Palestine, the point that Jesus makes is universally applicable. The Gospel is to be the central preoccupation of preaching and evangelization. Everything else is secondary. Of course the completion of evangelization is a new moment, after which the separate skills of teaching and organization are important. It is tempting to let the dynamics of organization and structure overtake the essential apostolic mission of every parish. Just as the excesses of power skewed David's fidelity to the covenant, so the excesses of organizational behavior can blur a Christian's vision of his or her own essential mission which is to reflect the Lord Jesus.

Point

The purpose of the community Jesus founded is not organizational perfection but the extension of His work to the world outside and the world within.

FRIDAY — Fourth Week of the Year
Si 47:2-11   *Mk 6:14-29*

First Reading

This reading from an Old Testament hymn in praise of David, written centuries after his death, reveres David not as he actually was but as he was remembered. The reign of David marks the highwater point of Israel's biblical story. It was a Camelot moment when Israel was at the peak of her political and military glory. The memory of David evokes powerful emotions in the Jewish soul. This song of unrestrained hero worship remembers David's victory over Goliath, his reverence for the ark and the divine promise of an eternal dynasty. From Saul's pathetic debacle at Mount Gilboa, David brought Israel to a dazzling height. This eulogy extracts the heart of David's meaning for Israel's history. In these same ways, the Messiah would be another David: He would defeat the enemy, bring fresh vigor to the worship of God and establish an unending community. This is how the Messiah would be a son of David.

Gospel Reading

This is the only event described in Mark's Gospel that does not center on Jesus. In this story of John the Baptist, we see some early efforts at trying to understand Jesus' identity. The story quickly flashes back to the details of the Baptist's execution at the behest of Herod's paramour. Christian tradition has distilled the significance of John as the precursor of Jesus. But he was also a baptizer and a prophet in his own right. John spoke God's Word to his contemporaries. He spoke of repentance, covenant living and the need to prepare for the kingdom. John was a faithful prophet properly claimed by both Testaments. With John's death, we see the shadow of impending death cross Jesus' ministry for the first time. David and John were centuries apart. Yet, each in his own way has influenced our understanding of Jesus.

Point

The songs of David and the message of John live on in our liturgy and in our image of Jesus. We also influence the image of Jesus which the next generation will have.

SATURDAY — Fourth Week of the Year
1 K 3:4-13   *Mk 6:30-34*

First Reading

This reading emphasizes the most famous attribute of Solomon—his wisdom. This is our first introduction to his reign as he prays for an understanding heart. In many ways, this is the prayer of every age. An understanding heart is not locked into prejudice and unexamined assumptions, but is able to step out of its own psychological house to empathize with others. Such an ability is in good measure a gift which we have traditionally called "wisdom."

Furthermore, an unprecedented amount of information floods in upon us every day through all kinds of media. With such an informational overload, many of us have a deep uncertainty about the larger picture: the roots of our being and the core issues of life. We do not need more data as much as we need the insight to see how it hangs together. The "why" of life and history is an elusive target.

Gospel Reading

Mark describes the enormous crowds that gathered to hear Jesus. The Lord did not give them new information about the physical universe: no new physics, chemistry or biology. What Jesus imparted was wisdom—the why of life and of history. Thus, His message is a message of liberation. To the familiar experiences of life, love and law, Jesus brings a context, a new Gestalt, a wider perspective. For this reason, His message is not bound to any culture or era. It speaks a universal message.

Point

The Gospel belongs to no political, economic or ideological viewpoint. It is a message of wisdom that teaches us how to live in love, die in peace and experience an eternal kind of life.

MONDAY — Fifth Week of the Year
1 K 8:1-7, 9-13   *Mk 6:53-56*

First Reading

This week, we will examine the reign of Solomon—a man whose image far exceeds his actual performance. Although he was a king of enormous material accomplishments for Israel, he fatally neglected to nurture stability and unity among the tribes. Today's reading describes the moment when the ark was brought forward into the temple which Solomon finally had built. When the ark was carried inside, the glory of the Lord filled the temple in an Old Testament sign of God's presence. The First Book of Kings gives extensive descriptions of the temple furnishings, its cedar beams and majestic walls. Within this ornate temple, exceeded in splendor only by Solomon's palace, the primitive ark was enshrined to remind people that they were a people of the covenant. The magnificence of the temple, however, shifted the consciousness of the people. Attention became focused less on covenant than on temple ritual, temple regulations, temple personnel. Gradually, the ark became closely identified with the Solomonic regime, more a symbol of the monarchy than of the covenant.

Gospel Reading

Mark summarizes Jesus' ministry of healing and teaching. We can contrast the fulsome splendor of the reign of Solomon with the simplicity of Jesus. To all appearances, Jesus was a wandering teacher. Yet, all the glory of God, the wisdom traditionally attributed to Solomon and the power of the covenant were all contained in Jesus. Jesus was the reality toward which the entire temple ritual and majesty were pointing. He embodied what all of it was for—God healing mankind.

Point

Not even Solomon with all his splendor could heal a single soul of sin. Healing and life are at the center of religion.

TUESDAY — Fifth Week of the Year
1 K 8:22-23, 27-30   *Mk 7:1-13*

First Reading

Solomon's prayer expresses the initial meaning and spiritual thrust of the temple. This is perhaps the most magnificent moment of his life as he puts into words the significance of the temple and of any church building. It was to be a house of prayer. Although no place on earth can contain the God of the universe, the temple is a place where people can give public and community expression to the personal faith that binds them together. If a person sins, he or she can come to the temple to pray. If a foreigner from a distant land comes here, he or she will meet God. This is a powerful vision of the temple as a place for spiritual renewal and the revival of the world. We see what became of this great vision in today's Gospel reading.

Gospel Reading

We see the debasing of a magnificent tradition in today's Gospel reading. The Pharisees had devised a number of ways to circumvent the Law. They had so managed to gut the meaning of the Law that it would never seriously influence secular affairs. They had made its observance easy and pointless. Instead of the difficult business of working for basic justice, they preoccupied themselves with cleaning cups and washing hands. Jesus came to bring new life to a spiritual tradition first given expression in Solomon's temple prayer but which had by now grown old and weary. Jesus insists that the kind of game to which the Pharisees had reduced the Law could never give life. They were using this collection of conventions to avoid the clear meaning of the Law.

Point

The Gospel is not primarily the source of a new legal system, but a way to make contact with the power of Easter.

WEDNESDAY — Fifth Week of the Year
1 K 10:1-10   *Mk 7:14-23*

First Reading

During Solomon's reign, a fantastic flowering of culture occurred. It was a time of great national pride when scholars began to collect the great traditions that eventually came down to us in the Old Testament. It was a time when Solomon used Israel's strategic geographic position on the trade routes to generate enormous wealth through granting franchises and licenses. He greatly expanded Israel's international trade. The queen of Sheba (Yemen) came to Solomon to hear his wisdom and probably to talk business. This meeting lent itself to all kinds of conjecture. The former royal family of Ethiopia claimed descent from Solomon through the queen of Sheba. Although their "affair" is apocryphal, her visit indicates the extent to which Solomon had opened the borders of Israel to membership in the community of nations. The wealth, however, did not trickle down. His splendid and dazzling display was resting on a very fragile foundation of oppression and growing division in the land.

Gospel Reading

The Lord states that nothing we eat can make us impure. Mark's recollection of these words shows us how traumatic it was for the early Church to appreciate the genuine liberation Jesus had brought them from the constrictions of the Law. Permitting the consumption of hitherto unclean foods must have been a difficult emotional experience for them. Mark shows us how Jesus rendered all foods clean. If nothing from the outside can make us evil, then nothing from the outside can impose holiness upon us. Spiritual renewal must come from within. Outward displays of religiosity cannot compensate for the lack of transformation within. This was the exact critique the Lord made of Pharisaic religion.

Point

Outward secular or religious splendor cannot replace covenant living. It is the rock on which everything else is built.

THURSDAY — Fifth Week of the Year
1 K 11:4-13   *Mk 7:24-30*

First Reading

The internal fault lines of Solomon's reign begin to appear. There was more than idolatry to his life. He discovered that he was spending a great deal more than he was taking in. His solution to the deficit problem was to force the people of Israel into slave labor for a third of every year to continue his public works projects. He overtaxed the artisans; he imposed corrupt governors over the people; he created a standing army and navy; he collected a mammoth harem as much for image and alliance-building as for personal satisfaction. This gigantic collection of Gentile concubines imported their religions with them into Israel. The reason for the biblical judgment against Solomon was that by mixing with pagans, Israel was neglecting the covenant. Now, Solomon presides in his old age over a collapsing kingdom that will survive only as long as he does. After him, the deluge. Because the prophets had so consistently attributed Israel's collapse to dalliance with pagans, contact with Gentiles became a social and religious taboo.

Gospel Reading

The taboo against association with Gentiles adds greater

meaning to today's Gospel reading. This scene with the Syro-Phoenician woman is extraordinary in several respects. First, she is Gentile. Secondly, she is a woman. Jesus has no hesitation in speaking with her on either count. Thirdly, she asks Jesus for healing at a distance, which He does effortlessly and for the first time in Mark's Gospel. Mark is suggesting that Jesus' power was not reducible to any one of the then prevalent forms of a "magic touch." Finally, she recognizes the historical distinction in God's plan between Jew and Gentile which Jesus now transcends. This justified the outreach of the Church at Antioch and Rome to the Gentiles. Throughout Mark's Gospel, we see Jesus breaking taboos—against lepers, a woman with a flow of blood, unclean foods and now a Gentile woman.

Point

We need a strong sense of identity as Christians to effectively reach out to others. This requires not only a strong devotional life, but an active liturgical life to celebrate our common faith.

FRIDAY — Fifth Week of the Year
1 K 11:29-32; 12:19   *Mk 7:31-37*

First Reading

Rebellion is in the air. The prophet Ahijah is a conservative revolutionary from Shiloh, the ancient religious home in the north of the old tribal confederacy. He dramatizes his prophecy that the northern tribes will split away from Judah in the South after Solomon's death by chopping up his cloak. Under Solomon, the tribes were required to supply food, labor and money for the state. They were overtaxed and overburdened. When representatives of the North complained to Solomon's son,

Rehoboam, whom the Book of Sirach characterizes as a "fool" (47:23), he made the fatal mistake of punitively increasing their burden. With that insensitive act, the northern tribes broke away and selected Jeroboam as king. The split would never again be healed.

Gospel Reading

Jesus is in the Gentile district of the Decapolis—the Ten Cities. His healing of the deaf man is a parable in action similar to Ahijah's. Not only does Jesus enable us to hear God's Word, but to hear it as addressed to us. He enables us to hear the sounds of the poor and needy, and to be attuned to the difficulties of our fellow human beings. The people in the Gospel reading remarked upon how completely Jesus fulfilled the prophecies of healing the deaf and the mute found in Isaiah (35:5). The deeper meaning of that old prophecy of Isaiah was more than a prediction of mended auricular problems. The Messiah would enable people to deal with each other on a more sensitive level and would make us aware of the fragile web of relationships and respect that hold a community together. To hear and speak on this level is a sign of the era of the Messiah.

Point

Rehoboam was deaf to the sounds of oppression and discontent around him. His disability was not in his ears but in his heart.

SATURDAY — Fifth Week of the Year
1 K 12:26-32; 13:33-34   *Mk 8:1-10*

First Reading

When the split between North and South became final, Solomon's son, Rehoboam, ruled the southern kingdom of

Judah. Jeroboam, an independently wealthy former staff officer of Solomon, ruled the northern kingdom called Israel. From this point, each region will develop its own traditions, prophets and heroes. David and Solomon had so successfully fused politics and religion in the Jerusalem Temple that Jeroboam concluded it would be political suicide to allow people from the North to continue to go there. He set about establishing an alternative northern ritual with its own shrines, altars, priests and festivals to replace the Jerusalem Temple. This is one of the roots of the Samaritan separation from and antipathy toward the Jerusalem Jews. In return, the Jews of Judah would look upon them as rebels and semi-pagans. With this reading, we will leave a divided North and South for a while.

Gospel Reading

Jesus feeds four thousand. Mark uses this miracle at the conclusion of Jesus' ministry in Gentile territory to show the gift of the Eucharist to be for Gentiles as well as Jews. Multiplications of bread are classic Gospel symbols of the Eucharist. Mark's Gospel describes two such miracles: one for the Jews and another for the Gentiles. Jesus does here in symbol what He will later do in act—His body broken and His blood spilled for all people: communists, atheists, Islamic fundamentalists, abortionists. Jesus lived and died for everyone.

Point

The Eucharist should heal and not create divisions.

MONDAY — Sixth Week of the Year
Jm 1:1-11   *Mk 8:11-13*

First Reading

For the next few weeks, we will read New Testament letters that describe the building and consolidation of the early

Church. These letters from James, Jude, Peter and the letter to Timothy track the transformation of the early apocalyptic fervor surrounding the last days into an enduring Christian life style in this world. We will see the early Church grappling with the application of the Christian faith to everyday life.

The Letter of James, written by a leader of the early Church, seems to be a Christian version of the Old Testament Wisdom literature. It is a collection of common sense principles of Christian living. Instead of soaring visions, speculative metaphysics and conceptual breakthroughs, James describes "nuts and bolts" Christianity. In this first reading, he addresses not the fire of persecution but the ordinary problems and trials that are part of every person's life. James makes an assertion that initially strikes us as strange. He indicates that difficulties can be catalysts of spiritual maturity as well as ways of our experiencing firsthand the death and Resurrection of Christ. Just as a person insulated from problems will become emotionally and psychologically stunted, so the absence of challenge can trap an individual into perpetual spiritual adolescence. Suffering cleanses and toughens faith.

Gospel Reading

The Pharisees look for a heavenly sign as evidence of Jesus' qualifications. Jesus refuses such a display for them. The most powerful sign He presented to them was the pattern of His life and teaching. If they failed to see God at work there, no heavenly spectacular would convince them.

Point

Christians are not problem-free. The sign we offer our world is a faith that sustains us in good times and bad.

TUESDAY — Sixth Week of the Year
Jm 1:12-18   *Mk 8:14-21*

First Reading

Yesterday, James described difficulties in our public lives that are not of our own making. In this reading, he discusses events and feelings within us over which we have no immediate control. We are not complete masters in our own house. James locates the source of sin in a primal disorder we all carry around. The stab of jealousy, the crease of hatred or the darker passions that surge from some dark center within us can be triggered by almost anything. Left unguarded, such isolated sentiments have their own momentum. Dark emotions coalesce into a frame of mind; a disposition expresses itself in actions; actions merge into habits; habits lead to spiritual death. But the Word is also implanted within us with its own life-cycle. Emotions of forgiveness or concern also form a frame of mind that can concretize itself into good habits and spiritual vitality. We are not helpless and passive bystanders in a cosmic struggle between good and evil. The arena of conflict is within ourselves.

Gospel Reading

Jesus warns His disciples against being infected by the skepticism and cynicism of the Pharisees who had turned religion into a game. He uses the disciples' physical hunger to speak of a deeper spiritual hunger that can be satisfied by the Eucharist. The eucharistic celebration that gives us spiritual nourishment is more than the reception of communion. It is hearing the Word, gathering with fellow-Christians, renewing our common covenant with the Lord, identifying our lives with the death and Resurrection of Jesus and receiving from the one bread and cup—this entire ensemble of moments provides the strength we need for our spiritual journey.

Point

Faithful celebration of the Eucharist works its own miracle in our lives. The miracle of conversion is the gradual turning from death to a life that is deathless.

WEDNESDAY — Sixth Week of the Year
Jm 1:19-27   *Mk 8:22-26*

First Reading

This is a well-known section of James' letter about the place of Scripture in our lives. Listening to the Word, as preached or written, can become sterile unless we wrestle it into concrete shape in our lives. Extensive study of Scripture and familiarity with the conclusions of modern scholarship are no substitutes for putting the Word into practice. There is no transforming power in Scripture that is merely heard, memorized, quoted or analyzed. James compares such an approach to a quick glance at a mirror that is easily forgotten.

The early Church Fathers saw divine meaning and a specific message in virtually every comma of Scripture. Today, we place greater emphasis on the human and cultural intermediaries of God's scriptural Word. Still, it is important not to lose the reverence for the biblical Word as God's message to us today.

Gospel Reading

We have an odd miracle in today's Gospel reading. This is the first blind man to be healed in Mark's Gospel. He

symbolizes the spiritual blindness of the disciples who consistently failed to see Jesus' meaning as in yesterday's Gospel
reading. This is the only miracle in the Gospels that is gradual.
The progressive restoration of the man's sight indicates the
gradual appreciation of Jesus by His followers. Part of Mark's
genius is his ability to lead the reader along the same path of
cumulative insight that those first disciples experienced. It can
be a very moving and powerful spiritual experience to read the
entire Gospel of Mark prayerfully in a single sitting.

Point

*The Word of God comes to life if we let it intersect our
deepest concerns.*

THURSDAY — Sixth Week of the Year
Jm 2:1-9   *Mk 8:27-33*

First Reading

James moves rapidly among a variety of subjects not only
to accommodate the attention span of his readers but also
because Wisdom literature tends to link loosely disconnected
observations about the business of living. The subject of this
reading is favoritism—the cyanide of family, parish or community life. James points to a possibly real but probably
hypothetical instance of two contrasting individuals entering a
church. There is an inveterate human tendency to fawn over
the person who looks successful and to dismiss the poorly
dressed as inconsequential. James cautions us not to be so
summary in our classification of others. Appearances are easily
manufactured and more frequently hide than reveal the insides
of a person. To love those who are young, wealthy and attractive is easy. It requires no Gospel, no Spirit, no Word to urge us

to do so. But to express the love of the Lord to those who are on the margins of society and popularity is difficult. It is precisely for this that we need the empowerment of the Gospel, Spirit and Word.

Gospel Reading

This is the axis of Mark's Gospel. The blindness of the disciples is gradually removed as Peter recognizes Jesus as the Messiah. Upon that initial insight the Lord begins to explain that the Messiah must suffer and die to bring about the kingdom. For the first time in Jewish consciousness, Jesus joins the notions of the Messiah and the mysterious Suffering Servant of Isaiah. From this moment, all the separate prophecies will begin to tumble together to show who Jesus really is. It is this particular conjunction of salvation and suffering that fuels Christianity's option on the side of the poor. The Lord continues to be especially present to them as must be the Church. While we work to eliminate misery, we know that pain has enormous power to open us to God's grace. The passion of Christ is repeated in thousands of lives every day. Maybe through us, some of these people can begin to experience His Resurrection as well.

Point

To turn away from the "losers" of society is human. To embrace them is divine.

FRIDAY — Sixth Week of the Year
Jm 2:14-24, 26   *Mk 8:34-9:1*

First Reading

Are we saved by the intensity of our personal religious experience or by the conduct of our lives? In his letter to the

Romans, Paul sees Abraham's faith as decisive. In this first reading, James points to the kind of life Abraham lived as critical. A fundamental question of Christian theology is whether salvation is, in any sense, earned by our good works. Around the answer to that question have been built libraries, professional careers, theological cultures and traditions. We can descend from the great issue of justification by faith to a simpler application. Faith and life style are mutually related. Our life is a practical expression of our faith. An avowed agnostic who lives a life of sensitive service to others might well have more faith than he or she would articulate. The reverse is also true. How a person lives might indicate a deeper lack of faith and love than he or she would admit.

Gospel Reading

Jesus describes the implications of a suffering Messiah. Suffering can quicken the growth of the kingdom of God. The intersection of suffering and glory in Jesus' life was not simply a quirk of Jewish history or of the obduracy of these particular Jewish leaders. The connection derives from the way the world works. As long as sin pervades our world and its social structures, the friction of sin and grace will continue. The followers of Jesus must not only be prepared to be countercultural but to endure psychic, economic and even physical pain for their discipleship. Suffering has so pervasive and critical a place not because God enjoys suffering but because the drag of sin is so extensive and massive that we can release ourselves from its inertia only with great and painful effort.

Point

The suffering we are willing to endure, and not our theological knowledge, is the most telling proof of the depth of our faith.

SATURDAY — Sixth Week of the Year
Jm 3:1-10   *Mk 9:2-13*

First Reading

The subject is the grandeur and power of words. Words have force. They can whip a crowd into a frenzy or turn a mob into a congregation. They can win elections and destroy careers. Words can comfort, heal, disturb, incite and wound. Words can be seeds of discontent, suspicion and ill-will. Words, or the "tongue" as James describes it, are the seeds we scatter in our world. Inevitably, they bring forward a harvest. A person can do more financial harm and personal injury to another by words strategically placed than by any physical assault. No idle piece of gossip is really harmless; no lie is completely white; kind words are not totally forgotten. Once uttered, words cannot be retrieved. Our language and conversation are ways we express what we are and what we love to others. Words can crucify Christ or transport His love to others.

Gospel Reading

The dominant role Jesus gave to suffering in His Messiahship must have been extremely depressing for the disciples. Their expectations had been nurtured by years of prophesied glory, honor and power. Memories of David swirled in their heads. After Jesus spoke of rejection and death, they needed strength. They needed Transfiguration. In a moment of great mystery and power, they experience the glory of Jesus as He stands between the Old Testament pillars of Moses and Elijah—the Law and the Prophets. Then they hear the voice. That single explosive experience showed these three disciples that Jesus' impending fate in Jerusalem was part of the ancient design of God to bring mankind back to the center. They realized as well that this would also be the path for them.

Point

Suffering and the kingdom come in many forms. Words can be instruments of either.

MONDAY — Seventh Week of the Year
Jm 3:13-18   *Mk 9:14-29*

First Reading

James explores the difference between wisdom and cunning. "Wisdom from above" is the use of our gifts and talents to build up the Body of Christ. It is know-how in the work of reconciliation and bridging differences. The wise man knows almost instinctively when to speak out and when to remain silent. Cunning, by contrast, is the cultivation of a virtuous appearance for self-promotion. It is the use of one's community, parish or family for one's own ambition. The word "cunning" might be replaced by euphemisms such as "competitiveness" and "aggressiveness." By any name, it transforms a community into a group of factions united only by self-interest. A church community is a place to put the service of all before everything else.

Gospel Reading

After the Transfiguration experience, Jesus continues His ministry by expelling an evil spirit from a boy. Inexplicably, the disciples had been unable to do so. Several points emerge from this incident. First, God's Son used His power to assist human beings. The same should be true for our gifts and abilities: they should be used to draw people together. Secondly, the expulsion of demons was never an easy process. Demons take many forms and cannot be expelled with formulas alone. To exorcise selfishness and hatred (rather than spectral infestation) from a community requires more than a magic word or technique. It calls for prayer and self-transformation. Finally, there are degrees of sin and of faith. The more faith-filled we are, the more power we have to change and assist those around us.

Point

Our gifts and graces are not private possessions.

TUESDAY — Seventh Week of the Year
Jm 4:1-10   *Mk 9:30-37*

First Reading

There is no substitute for repentance. James lists various disorders that can infect a community: envy, quarreling, infighting. Today, a huge array of methods exists to referee conflict and negotiate differences among groups. We can produce a passable peace or armistice in a parish or family by such devices. But the reconciliation that is curative requires repentance. Otherwise, technique becomes little more than a band-aid to assuage pain. It does not cut out the tumor. No management seminar can replace prayer and personal conversion. Deep unity is a gift of the Holy Spirit. The only true remedies for community division are repentance and forgiveness.

Gospel Reading

For a second time, Jesus repeats His prediction of coming suffering and pain. Some disciples continue to avoid the point as they argue about position and power. Jesus places a child in their midst to insist that position and power are not guarantees of genuine discipleship. In those days, a child had few rights.

Children were seen as little more than parental property. What the Lord is emphasizing is that care for the insignificant for the Gospel's sake is the touchstone of true discipleship. It is not title but service that distinguishes the follower of Christ.

Point

Repentance takes work. To seek reconciliation with those around us is the real opus Dei.

WEDNESDAY — Seventh Week of the Year
Jm 4:13-17   *Mk 9:38-40*

First Reading

In today's first reading, James urges perspective. To make a successful living and to achieve our professional goals are not trivial pursuits. We should place our projects, however, into the perspective of the larger purpose of our life. If we should not live with the illusion that our health and life can be indefinitely extended, then neither should we live in the shadow of death so that its inevitability deprives our life here of all meaning. "If the Lord wills it we shall live to do this . . ." In the space of time given us by the Lord, we are intended to play a part in bringing forth the kingdom. More important than the quantity of years a person is given is the quality of his or her life. After we die, the Spirit of God will continue to dwell among people as our world and species survive without us. But while we are here, He works through us.

Gospel Reading

Life is wasted by nurturing old wounds. We should give them a chance to heal. The kingdom is at our fingertips. To feed animosities is to drive the kingdom of God further beyond our grasp. Rather than drawing tight lines between people according to income level, nationality and ideology, we should look to the larger enterprise in which we are all engaged. Jesus tells us to unite ourselves with people of good will wherever they are. Many people who do not carry the name of Catholic or Christian have devoted their lives toward goals related to our own. We should not blind ourselves to these deeper ties that bind huge sectors of the human race.

Point

Differences are easy to create. Hundreds of them are generated every day in schoolyards, homes and offices across the nation. It is more difficult to find the lines of unity among people.

THURSDAY — Seventh Week of the Year
Jm 5:1-6   Mk 9:41-50

First Reading

James appeals to a stereotype of the wealthy person, a kind of early editorial cartoon image. He pictures a person who has acquired wealth and success at the expense of others and whose short-run success has left him or her spiritually bankrupt. The good left undone, the concern unexpressed, the needs unmet, the pain unrelieved, the wounds left unhealed all become the ghostly inventory of a spiritually wasted life. James refers to the mechanics of an individual's rise to power and wealth. The means we use to attain our goals make us what we are as much as the ends we pursue.

Gospel Reading

Today's Gospel reading is about a balance sheet of sorts.

Jesus asks us to compare the eternal destiny we choose with the short-run comforts we experience in this life. The pursuit of pleasure, power or money at any price can destroy our capacity for love and faith. It affects the kind of people we become. The kind of existence we will have after death is defined by our life here. If we have suffocated our hearts by greed and hate, the Lord will say to us at the final judgment, "Very well. That is what you will be forever!" We call this hell. If we have spent our lives in efforts of love and hope, the Lord will say, "That is what you shall be forever!" This we call heaven. In each case, the choice is ours to make in this life.

Point

Material accumulation cannot satisfy the built-in desire of every human being for the goods of the Spirit: love, faith and hope.

FRIDAY — Seventh Week of the Year
Jm 5:9-12   *Mk 10:1-12*

First Reading

James calls for patience. The various pieces of advice he gives throughout this letter cohere in the light of faith. They are not formulas for a quick fix, for immediate results. The patterns of activity in which we have been engaged have created deep tracks and habits that are not easily dislodged. Perhaps, James' counsel of patience might seem dilatory in our culture so accustomed to rapid resolution of problems. Any significant human achievement of substance requires effort and painful work. The same is true of the spiritual life. To achieve, for example, the clarity and simplicity of life where our word is known to be dependable requires great effort in the present climate of the workplace. To be such a person is a great achievement.

Gospel Reading

As Jesus continues His ministry, the subject of marriage arises. To the Jewish practice of prevalent and easy male divorce of women, Jesus refers to the Book of Genesis as evidence of God's original intention for marriage. Man and woman are to be united in an indestructible bond of love for life. In our century, this is an unusually difficult Gospel pronouncement. Marriage has never been easy but in a climate of socially acceptable and facile divorce, a text like this demands heroic effort. It fits especially well into the controlling theme of Mark's Gospel: suffering as a mark of true discipleship. To make a marriage relationship work requires a great deal of effort and pain. It demands a recurrent process of reconciliation.

Point

A vibrant and effective spiritual life is not automatic. It is the result of effort, planning and sacrifice.

SATURDAY — Seventh Week of the Year
Jm 5:13-20   *Mk 10:13-16*

First Reading

We come to the conclusion of James' letter as he speaks about the anointing of the sick. This is the text used by the Council of Trent as the scriptural warrant for the Sacrament of Anointing. At one time, this sacrament was administered as "extreme unction" to a person at the point of death. Today we celebrate it to make the Church's prayer of faith available to anyone who is seriously ill. James speaks about the effect of this prayer of faith. It inserts the physical or emotional suffering of a person into the priestly prayer of Jesus. There is no more dramatic instance of the continuation of Jesus' ministry to the sick than is this sacrament when properly celebrated. Our prayer reclaims the ill person from despair and gives new hope and assurance of the loving power of God. It reminds people that God has not abandoned them in their time of pain.

Gospel Reading

As the disciples ward off children from Jesus' presence, we have Mark's single reference to the indignation of Jesus. The disciples were excluding those who seemed to matter least. Unlike our day, children had no special place of respect in Semitic society. Jesus especially insists that these children be allowed to approach Him. When people are ill and seem to have lost their productivity and usefulness in our status conscious society, the Lord calls them especially to Himself. He wishes to be near to them particularly in the Sacrament of Anointing.

Point

Our moments of distress are times when the Lord seeks to be closest to us.

MONDAY — Eighth Week of the Year
1 P 1:3-9

Mk 10:17-27

First Reading

The First Letter of Peter, like that of James, was written to a Christian community coming to grips with living no longer in the shadow of the end of the world but as part of an organized and ongoing society. The people he addresses were a religious minority who, though not officially persecuted, were objects of growing hostility from their neighbors. Peter writes to them about the challenge of patient Christian living without the thrill of dramatic spiritual ecstasies. He encourages these second-generation Christians to trust their sacramental experience of the Lord. That sacramental experience draws its genuinity and guarantee from Jesus' Resurrection. The clash between our Christian way of living and the prevailing culture creates a tension which is felt by every serious Christian. That tension tests our faith like a refining fire that burns off whatever is flabby, romantic and childish, leaving behind a tough, adult, serious faith. The resulting matured faith becomes our living link to the Lord.

Gospel Reading

Jesus describes an adult, serious faith in today's Gospel reading. To his response that he already follows the Commandments, the Lord instructs a young man to give away his property. His refusal, the only one recorded in the Gospel, showed his inability to take this next step. In our search for spiritual maturity and depth, we must recall the important place of the Commandments. As simple as they are for any child to remember, they embody the essential foundation for Christian growth. Just as the Old Testament was the foundation for the New, so the sense of justice embodied in the Decalogue is the precondition for adult love. Without a sound sense of justice, love becomes flaccid, permissive and destructive. In the same way, even though the covenant living described in the Commandments is not specifically Christian, it provides the foundation upon which Christian perfection is built.

Point

Our faith is tested and deepened not in a classroom but by life.

TUESDAY — Eighth Week of the Year
1 P 1:10-16   *Mk 10:28-31*

First Reading

Peter stresses to these second-generation Christians that because they have not been able to see Jesus in the flesh does not mean they are second-rate Christians. Our sacramental experience of Christ is genuine and real. This sacramental Christian experience of the Lord is the fulfillment of the Old Testament prophetic message. Peter goes on to say that Jesus is the fulfillment of every person's religious search. Because the experience of the Lord is so fundamental, we must adjust our lives to revolve around it or else we will lose it. Just as Jesus is the center of human history, so is He the center of our lives. If we place anything else at the center, our lives will tilt off balance.

Gospel Reading

Jesus describes the reward for those who have given everything up to follow Him. He speaks by implication as well to those who have dedicated everything they have to the service of His Lordship. He uses Semitic exaggeration to say that these will receive a gift of God's presence qualitatively superior to anything they have surrendered. This is the fulfillment of that deepest part of ourselves where we carry the image of God. The Lord's words will strike no responsive chord in those who have never bothered to enter within themselves to see the trace of God. To people who have cluttered up their lives with possessions and synthetic pleasures, the notion of an eternal existence without such surroundings is as foreign as is Palm Springs to an associate pastor.

Point

The balance, depth and authenticity of our lives depend on what we choose as our center.

WEDNESDAY — Eighth Week of the Year
1 P 1:18-25   *Mk 10:32-45*

First Reading

Peter illustrates Christ's meaning for us not only from the fulfillment of prophecy but from Jesus' own pain. He uses a commercial metaphor to indicate that we were, in effect, repurchased from the slavery of sin not by money but by the life and death of Jesus. To have been redeemed or "bought back" means that we once belonged to another—we were under the control of evil. But Jesus' death and Resurrection have placed us under the control of the Spirit. The entire brutal history of mankind is the story of that original bondage and of those who, once redeemed, have sold themselves back into spiritual slavery. That we have the awesome choice to do so is itself a gift of the Resurrection.

Gospel Reading

As He approaches Jerusalem, Jesus describes for a third time the suffering He will have to endure. In the Gospel of Mark, Jerusalem is portrayed as the center of hostility to Jesus. It embodied the corrupt political and religious forces that had conspired to kill Him. It also embodied what Judaism could have become. Again, the disciples miss the Lord's point. They skip the suffering and look forward to the promised glory. The Lord insists that the suffering would not simply be a temporary earthly stage to earthly glory. Rather, the pain of this life (and perhaps throughout this life) is a preliminary to the glory that will be ours in the life beyond this one. Where the disciples think in chronological stages, Jesus speaks of personal levels of existence. For now, greatness is measured by service to others. The true measure of spiritual greatness will be our willingness to imitate not the triumphant and glorious Lord but the Jesus who lovingly and decisively now moves forward to Jerusalem to give His life for all.

Point

To continue Peter's commercial metaphor, Jesus has paid the price. Now, we work to take delivery from an unwilling seller. Jesus has given us the power to rescue mankind from the power of evil.

THURSDAY — Eighth Week of the Year
1 P 2:2-5, 9-12   *Mk 10:46-52*

First Reading

This first reading contains several magnificent images of the Christian life. Like babies eager for food, we should be eager for spiritual nourishment. We should search out during the week whatever will build up our faith and trust in the Lord, because our diversions are not irrelevant to our faith. The Word is like a seed within us that we must cultivate. Its care requires patience and skill.

Through our baptism we form a Temple, an edifice of the

Spirit, constructed not as a static aggregate of souls but as a dynamic structure constantly being built from human lives. Like a church building that stands in a forest of skyscrapers, the presence of Christians in the world reminds our contemporaries of a deeper dimension to life. We are living proof that the realm of the Spirit is real. We are a priesthood linking God and our world.

Gospel Reading

This healing of blind Bartimaeus is the last healing in Mark's Gospel and the first time that a public proclamation of Jesus as Son of David is not silenced. The blindness of Bartimaeus was ocular; ours and that of the disciples so often is spiritual. The Lord enables us all to see if we want to see. Faith is given to those who seek it. This particular miracle sets the scene for the triumphal entry into Jerusalem where the people will again acclaim Jesus as Son of David and not be silenced. The final moments of Jesus' earthly ministry and of the great expression of His Messiahship on Calvary are approaching.

Point

Suffering does not give meaning to life. The kind of life we live gives meaning to suffering. Jesus' life gave clear meaning to Calvary.

FRIDAY — Eighth Week of the Year
1 P 4:7-13   *Mk 11:11-26*

First Reading

Peter emphasizes the community dimension of Christian living in a non-Christian society. Not only do we have an obligation to use our gifts for the service of others; we also need to allow others to bring forth their gifts. We all have an enabling ministry toward each other. Every community, despite the best of its intentions, experiences a trial by fire that tests its love and faith. Every community is given all the gifts it needs to enable it to thrive in spiritual power. So often, for a variety of political or economic reasons, these gifts are not released. "In all of you, God is to be glorified through Jesus Christ." The hope-filled message of Peter is that whatever differences and difficulties might exist among a group of Christians, the birth of genuine community is always possible. With prayer and the effort of love, it is probable.

Gospel Reading

The lectionary has omitted the Lord's triumphal entry into Jerusalem. This reading takes us directly to the final period of Jesus' life as He walks freely about the city and countryside. The curse of the fig tree is a prophetic action of Jesus. The tree is a symbol of the way religion had been politicized and trivialized over the years. The cleansing of the Temple is a second prophetic action. The rage of Jesus is directed past this small group of religious entrepreneurs toward the overall displacement of the fundamental purpose of the Law and covenant by secondary concerns and regulations. As the fig tree withered, so would this religious establishment die; as the Temple was cleansed, so would a renewed and reinvigorated people of God be born from the blood of the cross.

Point

Difficulties can cause us to rearrange our lives in an Easter rebirth.

SATURDAY — Eighth Week of the Year
Jude 17, 20-25   *Mk 11:27-33*

First Reading

The short letter of Jude is a reminder that we must fight to
keep faith vibrant. Like the letters of James and Peter, Jude
comes from a time when the early Church was staking out the
boundaries of its public identity. The urgent belief in the immediate return of the Lord had given way to an effort to live that
faith in a more stable and sustained spiritual environment. The
articulated content of belief began to take center stage. The
problem which Jude addresses is not persecution from outsid-
ers but corrosion from subversives within. At different points in
the letter, he calls them "worms," "blotches on the Christian
banquet," "grumblers," and "whiners." Clearly, this was not
an age of dialogue. Jude does stand for the important proposi-
tion that there are doctrines, positions and life styles which the
Christian community cannot assimilate or tolerate if it wishes to
retain its identity as the community of Jesus Christ. The boundaries of that tolerance may contract or expand over time. By
what it accepts and refuses to accept, the community makes a
public statement of its faith which itself is a witness to the
world.

Gospel Reading

Jesus' quizzical response to the interrogations of the
Pharisees deals more with their attitude than with their specific
questions. The setting is important. The hostility, cynicism and
constant cross-examination by the Pharisees had, by now,
become a constant drumbeat of Jesus' life. Here, He approaches the final hours of His life. The healings, teachings and
explanations have had no positive impact on these teachers of
the Law. They simply refused to believe. Their questions were

not inquiries but tools of harassment. Jesus responds by asking them a question that would force them to take a public stand about John the Baptist, an enigmatic and popular figure. They refuse.

Point

There comes a point when critique and examination must give birth to decision.

MONDAY — Ninth Week of the Year
2 P 1:2-7   *Mk 12:1-12*

First Reading

The Second Letter of Peter, one of the latest writings of the New Testament, is an effort to restore to second generation Christians a sense of urgency in their living the Christian faith by re-emphasizing the imminent return of the Lord. The sense of coming apocalypse began to diminish as the Christian community settled in. As these Christians incorporated themselves into the ongoing life of society, the fervor of their faith began to cool. This letter tries to restore the drive, ardor and spiritual "fire in the belly" that typified the first generation of believers. In today's reading, Peter is emphatic that through our baptism each of us has received all the spiritual equipment we need to live a life of heroic faith. He explains that the spiritual life has an expansive power of its own. Just as seemingly insignificant sins and failings can generate a progressive spiritual deterioration, so the act of faith can lead to virtue, discernment and personal self-mastery. This self-control becomes in turn the basis for perseverance, a solid prayer life and care for our fellow-Christians. Then it rises to love. It is a chain reaction or cumulative building process at which we must work by attending to ordinary things.

Gospel Reading

Many writers feel that this is the central parable of Mark's Gospel. It summarizes the basic conflict that underlies his entire Gospel story and the meaning of the ministry of Jesus. The vicious tenants refused to give their produce to the owner. The spiritual leaders of Jerusalem killed the various agents and prophets who had been sent to remind them of their position as tenants and not owners. Finally, they killed the Owner's Son as well, effectively rejecting the Owner. Yet, that act of savagery would become the start of a new vineyard, a new structure, a new covenant and a new people of God.

Point

Personal, social and spiritual success are not generated spontaneously or overnight. They are the result of cumulative work whose results are not to be hoarded but directed Godward.

TUESDAY — Ninth Week of the Year
2 P 3:12-15, 17-18   *Mk 12:13-17*

First Reading

Evidently, some people had ridiculed the notion of the end of the world. Peter affirms that the end of the world we know does not mean the extinction of all we have achieved. Whether the final scenario will be "fire or ice," God's purpose for the world will survive. The end will be followed by a new heaven and a new earth. Our certainty about the end is modified by the hope of transformation. Much of what we have done and created as Christians is too valuable to disappear in smoke. In some transcendent way, God will preserve the love and faith that have sustained millions over the centuries. Peter implies that we can hasten that end by our conduct. We have all heard and read about the ability of human beings to hasten the end of our planet. Peter speaks in another sense of our ability to hasten the emergence of God's final purpose for our world. We can do this by our conduct as Christians.

Gospel Reading

Jesus speaks to the Pharisees about the volatile subject of taxes. To give to Caesar what belongs to Caesar is not an admonition to isolate our political and civic life from our faith. Our Christian faith should permeate everything we do, including our lives as citizens. Because Christian viewpoints should not be absent from public policy discussions, it is no surprise that believers are involved in a variety of public issues, most notably those of abortion and the use of nuclear weaponry. The Lord is reminding the Pharisees and us that we do have civil obligations. We must perform them with the same care that we give to our religious duties.

Point

How and what we give to Caesar is a religious matter.

WEDNESDAY — Ninth Week of the Year
2 Tm 1:1-3, 6-12   *Mk 12:18-27*

First Reading

The Second Letter to Timothy is another guide to a Church very much in transition. It seems that the Twelve have died and the transmission of leadership in this wide-ranging collection of Christian communities was in the process of being institutionalized. Timothy is reminded to stir into a flame the Spirit of God he received not simply for preaching but for the faithful witness of the apostolic message. After the eyewitnesses of the life, death and Resurrection of the Lord were gone, authority passes to those who will faithfully transmit the original apostolic message. We are called as a community or parish to do the same. The Gospel entrusted to the Apostles and those first Christians has now been given to us to preserve not by embalming it but by living it.

Gospel Reading

Jesus speaks to the Sadducees about the next life. They did not believe in life after death and were, oddly enough from our perspective, the traditionalists of that era. The question they posed to Jesus was intended to make the entire concept of personal immortality look ridiculous by reference to the law of the Levirate marriage. Jesus recognizes their ploy and answers their grotesque, hypothetical question about a woman with seven husbands by asserting that the next life is not a simple extrapolation of life here. It is different in kind from what we have known here. Our personal identity survives because we continue as entire persons with love and concern for each other. Beyond that we cannot be more graphic. An excessive use of our imagination in explaining the mysteries of faith can lead to their trivialization.

Point

The promise of eternal life is a sacred message to every age. It is important that it is never trivialized or used for oblique political purposes.

THURSDAY — Ninth Week of the Year
2 Tm 2:8-15   *Mk 12:28-34*

First Reading

We have a snapshot of Paul in prison. Although Paul was put in chains, there is no imprisoning the Word of God because others will carry on the mission. The seed of the Word has been sown in people's hearts. We are only instruments of that larger and more certain work of the Holy Spirit. Paul quotes an early Christian song that if we die with Christ, we will also live with Him. The reference is not simply to the sacramental death and resurrection of baptism but also to our daily experience of success and failure. If we view our everyday experience in the light of the Lord, then the death and Resurrection of Christ will not be a remote and sacral event. It will embody a cycle that pervades the course of human life.

Gospel Reading

A teacher of the Law approaches Jesus with a typically academic question about the greatest of the commandments. Jesus responds by quoting the Book of Deuteronomy's demand for total love of God. He couples it with a command from Leviticus to love our neighbor as ourself. The distinctively Christian approach to the law and moral living is to place these two commands on an equal plane. They are not identical but equivalent. Distortion from the Christian model occurs when we emphasize one over the other. Maintaining that equilibrium is not easy. It is the function of prophets to recall us when we break the balance.

Point

To maintain the tension between the two great command-ments in our own lives is not easy. It requires regular self-examination.

FRIDAY — Ninth Week of the Year
2 Tm 3:10-17   *Mk 12:35-37*

First Reading

This exhortation to remain faithful looks to Scripture as a source of strength. The reference is to the Old Testament, for at this time the books of the New Testament were still being written and had not yet acquired the status of "Scripture." Sacred Scripture is not a collection of pious thoughts or memory verses. It is an expression of faith lived in a great variety of situations. Through the Old and New Testaments we see people in different cultures laboring to discern the presence of God in war and peace, illness and health, cultural elegance, popular depravity and political chaos. The Bible gathers for us a remarkable collection of testimonies to the faith not only of particular individuals but of entire peoples. Threaded throughout its books is a fundamental continuity of fidelity by and to the Lord. The contexts in which that faithfulness took shape differ little or markedly from our own. We remain in continuity with that fidelity not by blind imitation but by the effort to bring to life in our own time the faith and hope that characterized the people of the Bible.

Gospel Reading

Jesus affirms that Messiahship is not primarily a function of genetic descent from David. To be the Messiah is not essentially to be a Son of David according to the flesh. Instead, it is divine Sonship with a relationship to the Father far closer than David's. We become people of the Messiah to the extent that we try to copy Jesus' obedience to and intimacy with God in our own lives.

Point

A faithful son or daughter is not simply the result of a biological process. They are the result of a sharing of life and love.

SATURDAY — Ninth Week of the Year
2 Tm 4:1-8   Mk 12:38-44

First Reading

This injunction to faithful preaching of the Gospel has been called Paul's last testament. It is the eve of his martyrdom and the race is just about over. Just as Paul found many ways throughout his apostolate to drive home the Gospel message to audiences as different as the Thessalonians, Corinthians, Ephesians, Colossians, Romans and Galatians, so he charges Timothy to continue to preach the Gospel in a way that roots it in people's hearts. This is an ongoing charge to the Church. Intellectual styles change. Fidelity to the Gospel requires more than blind repetition. We must change to remain the same. If the core meaning of the Gospel is to be brought home to people in various cultures, the apostle must immerse himself or herself in the Catholic experience of the Lord to be able to express it in a way that will touch the mind and heart of any listener. Without such a basic experience of the Lord, one can collapse the Gospel without remainder into prevailing cultural fads or else speak the message in a vocabulary alien to everyone but ourselves. An apostle must stay in touch with the "street."

Gospel Reading

Our final reading from Mark's Gospel closes with a sharp contrast between the religious preening of the scribes and the humble, quiet faith of the poor widow. The difference between substance and appearance glares out at us. The scribes are the self-professed heirs of the Mosaic tradition while their studied display contradicts the heart of that tradition. The widow, on the other hand, unobtrusively places her few coins into the box in a gesture that links her with the holy ones of Israel over the centuries. She is the authentic embodiment of the Mosaic tradition.

Point

There is much more to fidelity than meets the eye.

MONDAY — Tenth Week of the Year
1 K 17:1-6   *Mt 5:1-12*

First Reading

We should recap events as we return this week to Israel's great national epic. The exodus from Egypt was followed by the savage period of the Judges and the institution of the kingship under Saul, David and Solomon. After Solomon's death, the kingdom broke apart into the rival states of Judah in the South and Israel in the North where Jeroboam was king. We rejoin the northern story a few generations later. Ahab, one of Jeroboam's successors, had married a Canaanite fanatic named Jezebel. She gradually worked to turn her native Canaanite fertility religion of Baal Melqart into the state religion by tearing down Israel's altars and persecuting Israelite prophets. Enter Elijah—a mysterious, eerie, awesome prophet of the North who bursts onto the scene dressed in hair garments and leather belt to crystallize opposition to Jezebel. In today's first reading, Elijah announces to King Ahab a three year drought to demonstrate the impotence of Baal Melqart as a fertility god and to prove that fruitfulness ultimately comes from the God of Israel. Then as suddenly as he arrives, Elijah, the challenger of conventional gods, departs.

Gospel Reading

In this most famous section of the teachings of Jesus that Matthew collected for us as the Sermon on the Mount, Jesus challenges conventional values in asserting that the poor in spirit, the lowly and persecuted are blessed. Where Luke's version of the Beatitudes speaks of the redemptive possibilities of real poverty, Matthew emphasizes a poverty of spirit applicable to all income brackets. Throughout this sermon, the Lord addresses attitudes. Often enough, our needs can force us to travel deep within ourselves to find spiritual resources which money cannot purchase. Poverty of spirit can be a true liberation when our identity and value are no longer wrapped up in the size of our bank account. Although poverty, need and public derision are not intrinsically sacramental, a person of faith can see in them a summons to a deeper and more interior Christian experience. Suffering can produce great agnostics as well as great saints. Faith makes the difference.

Point

The Creator God not only causes the earth to bring forth a harvest, but can also enable those at the margins of life to give birth to a rich and intense spiritual life.

TUESDAY — Tenth Week of the Year
1 K 17:7-16   *Mt 5:13-16*

First Reading

As the drought predicted by Elijah continues, he is sent to a widow at Zarephath in Sidon which is located in the pagan

Baal Melqart's homecourt. It was like the Pope going to Salt Lake City. Even here the drought had catastrophic effects. The widow and her ailing son were down to their last handful of flour and their final jar of oil which she shares with Elijah. For the kindness shown a prophet, she is rewarded by the God of Israel with a steady supply of food as well as the restoration of her son to health. The Gospels and the early Church saw a deep eucharistic background in this episode. This scene matches the impotence of the pagan fertility gods even among their followers with the power of the God of Israel toward someone who was not an Israelite. Even in pagan lands, God is in charge of the course of nature as well as of history.

Gospel Reading

Salt and light are used by Jesus as symbols of the important function we serve in the world. Salt improves, preserves and seasons something other than itself. Light brightens something other than itself. We are not to be a spiritual elite psychologically and culturally insulated from the surrounding world. By our words as well as our presence, we stand for an alternative value system as did Elijah. We remind the world of our God. Just as Elijah made the God of Israel known to the pagan woman, we make our Lord known by what we say and do.

Point

We serve the world most effectively not by isolation but through contact with and immersion in it.

WEDNESDAY — Tenth Week of the Year
1 K 18:20-39   Mt 5:17-19

First Reading

Elijah's confrontation with the pagan prophets is one of

the classic scenes of the Old Testament. Until now, there has
been a gradual and cozy blending of Israelite and pagan religious practices in the North. Jezebel's fanatical evangelism
brought the issue to a boiling point and forced a choice between the God of Israel and Baal Melqart. This contest on
Mount Carmel is high noon for the policy of syncretism that
had saturated the North. The test was to light the fire. The 450
prophets of Baal whipped and danced themselves into a frenzy
to excite their god into igniting the wood. Nothing happened.
Elijah ridiculed their whirling fury, suggesting sarcastically that
perhaps Baal Melqart had gone to the bathroom, was asleep or
on a business trip. Nothing continued to happen. Finally, the
exhausted pagan prophets stepped to the side. Elijah approached the woodpile and had it doused with water. With a
single prayer, a firebolt cracks out of the sky and lights the fire.
The people are awed and declare their singular devotion to the
God of Israel. Elijah then had the pagan prophets slain.

Gospel Reading

The Torah Law and covenant had been preserved with
great effort over the centuries from contamination. They were
sacred to the Jews. The precise and literal observance of the
Law and all of its secondary conventions had attained an
almost mantric quality that was thought to draw down the
blessing of God apart from the spirit in which that Law was
kept. Jesus refused to endow the Law with such sacral power.
Instead, He fulfilled its deepest intentions while being
pragmatic toward its etiquette. This recapture of the Law's
original purpose will be illustrated in the rest of the Sermon on
the Mount. The basic point the Lord makes is that the attitude
which obedience to the Law was intended to generate is more
determinative of our relationship with God than is the Law's
exact observance.

Point

Why we keep the Law is as important as our precision in keeping it.

THURSDAY — Tenth Week of the Year
1 K 18:41-46   *Mt 5:20-26*

First Reading

Because the combat on Mount Carmel proved the God of Israel superior to the pagan Baal Melqart, the drought has ended. Elijah demonstrated conclusively that Israel's God was the true God of fruitfulness. Now, he prays anxiously for the rain clouds to come. He waits for the divine promise to be fulfilled. At last, an aide sees a tiny cloud in the distance. In a moment of rare personal exultation, Elijah skips ahead of King Ahab's chariot to the royal compound at Jezreel. His running ahead during this 17 mile journey imitates the Oriental herald of victory celebrating and announcing the triumph of the God of Israel. The rain shower signified as well a new lease on spiritual life for the people of Israel. The people will never forget Elijah's triumph. Neither will Jezebel.

Gospel Reading

Jesus illustrates the deeper fulfillment of the Torah Law in the Sermon on the Mount through a series of six cases. The first instance He uses is that of murder. Society proscribes murder and punishes the murderer because this crime strikes viciously at the very heart of a civilized community. The Lord tells us that anger, abusive language and hatred can corrupt a community equally well. Anger can so dissolve the bonds of community that without a single act of murder ever occurring, the law of the jungle can seep into neighborhoods, courtrooms, public meetings, legislatures and families. In any real sense, such a community is dead. We can harm others in cunning ways as frightening as murder.

Point

We can take away or restore life to others in many ways.

FRIDAY — Tenth Week of the Year
1 K 19:9, 11-16　　　　　　　　　　　　　*Mt 5:27-32*

First Reading

The slaughter of her prophets and the miracle of the rain infuriated Jezebel. As she has Elijah hunted down, he escapes to a cave where he sits depressed and puzzled by this train of events. He had served God and done as he was told, yet in the wake of God's victory, he was now a fugitive. Elijah is told to await the Lord's coming. A marvelous revelation comes to him at Horeb (traditionally identified as Sinai). He looks to the earthquake and fire, the Exodus signs of God, but God was not in the terrible tremors of nature. Instead, God came in a gentle breeze, the spirit that lives in the prophet. Elijah is assured that God is present in the prophetic word. Assured of God's presence, he is told to prepare a successor for himself and for King Ahab. He had come back to one of the great places of Jewish memory to discover the presence of the same God in a different way. God was in the inner word, the gentle breeze; that gentle breeze began a revolution.

Gospel Reading

Jesus reminds us that although adultery can destroy a

marriage, lust in the heart or mind of a person can be just as devastating to a relationship. To preserve fidelity to a spouse or to God is not just a matter of what we do with our bodies. It also concerns what we do with our minds, feelings and hearts. Just as God was present in the simple words of the prophet Elijah, so the power to create, preserve or destroy a relationship is lodged inside ourselves. The spiritual bond of marriage can be destroyed in other ways than adultery. Infidelity begins in the mind.

Point

The great deeds of good and evil that find their way into history books are the end products of what takes place in the human mind and heart.

SATURDAY — Tenth Week of the Year
1 K 19:19-21   *Mt 5:33-37*

First Reading

Elisha becomes Elijah's disciple. He was from a wealthy family and was something of a gentleman farmer who knew of Elijah's exploits and wanted to serve the God of Israel. He responds to Elijah's summons by destroying his farm equipment and celebrating a farewell meal with his family and friends. That celebration signified the end of one part of his life and the beginning of another. It may have been that Elisha discovered a cause or purpose that pulled together all the ideals and feelings of unease that had plagued him. At any rate, the discovery of a true master was a time of celebration for him. We all have to live our own life but need not start a solitary search for the meaning of life. Apprenticeship to a master imparts a wisdom that we can eventually make our own. Elisha would succeed Elijah and continue the prophetic ministry very much in his own style. First, there was the need to learn from the master. Discipleship to a true master is not a slavery but a joy.

Gospel Reading

Jesus speaks to us of inner integrity. The Old Testament Law forbade the taking of false oaths. The lawyers had developed a number of ways to swear an oath that did not blaspheme nor fully bind. Instead of swearing by God, one could swear by heaven, earth, Jerusalem or by one's own self. All of these methods sounded sacred but were really ways of keeping your fingers crossed. The Lord cuts through all of this to say directly that the Law does not concern itself primarily with the literal truth of our words. We should not convey untruth at all. Obedience to the Law is not a game of words, mental reservations or legalisms. It does require that we be as good as our word. As disciples of the Lord, our everyday conversation should be so trustworthy that there is no need to bind ourselves by a special oath.

Point

Just as Elisha followed Elijah without reservation, so our discipleship to Jesus must be thorough. We cannot be sporadic disciples.

MONDAY — Eleventh Week of the Year
1 K 21:1-16   *Mt 5:38-42*

First Reading

The events surrounding Ahab's seizure of Naboth's vineyard are, after the drought, the second great event of Elijah's career. The details of this incident are simple and telling. Naboth owned a vineyard as part of his ancestral heritage. King Ahab wanted a garden park and became glum when Naboth would not sell to him. Jezebel resolved to obtain the vineyard for her husband. Naboth followed the traditional Israelite notion of land tenure in which the land belongs to God and was given to certain families for their custodial care to keep it fruitful. The land should stay in the family. Jezebel, on the other hand, had more mundane notions about land values. The commercial culture from which she came saw land simply as an investment vehicle, an item to be bought and sold. She intrigued successfully to have Naboth double-crossed and then executed. His vineyard was then seized by Ahab. This single act of injustice is enveloped by Ahab's broader repudiation of the traditional Israelite attitudes both as regards the land and the limited role of the ruler. Both were signs of pagan infiltration—Elijah's specialty.

Gospel Reading

Jesus also speaks about justice in today's Gospel reading. These difficult words from the Sermon on the Mount have lent themselves to all sorts of diverse interpretations. The general thrust of the Lord's words gives deeper meaning to the particular examples He uses. The Lord tells us that our conduct toward others should not be measured by legality alone. Our responsibilities before others in the sight of God are wider than those recognized by our legal system. Secondly, we should not seek precise equivalence in our dealings with others. We should not assist, lend to or favor others only to the exact extent they have done so for us. Our relationships with our fellow human beings should be governed by their need. Human relations need to be grounded on something deeper than a mathematical correlation of rights and duties.

Point

The Christian life is not an accounting sheet. Discipleship is a life of service measured by our capacity to give, as is the Lord's love for us.

TUESDAY — Eleventh Week of the Year
1 K 21:17-29   *Mt 5:43-48*

First Reading

Elijah confronts Ahab in a scene reminiscent of Nathan's confrontation with David. The institution of the prophet in Israel was special in its allowing a man of God to face down and question the policies and life style of the ruler, usually with impunity. Through Elijah, God pronounces judgment on Ahab for the wrong he had done to Naboth. Dogs will lick the blood of Ahab and Jezebel in an especially ignominious kind of death. After Ahab repents, however, the Lord forgives him and postpones the pronounced judgment against his dynasty. Jezebel did not repent and the prophecy was fulfilled in her case.

Gospel Reading

Forgiveness is difficult in any culture and for any person. Its real challenge is not moral but psychological. Essentially, it is a decision not to let the wrong done to us obstruct our future dealings with an individual. Very often, it takes a while for our emotions to catch up with the decision we have made. Forgiveness is a process. The alternative is to wallow in resentment which, once out of control, can color the rest of our lives. It is much the same when Jesus tells us to love our enemies. We should recall that the Sermon on the Mount was delivered to those who wanted to live under the reign of God. The Lord is explaining how that service of God shows itself in concrete ways. Love is also a decision. It is not the romantic attachment frequently portrayed in song and picture. It is an intelligent decision behind which our emotions may lag. To love an enemy is an assertive decision not to let another's hostility control my reaction. Love admits of degrees. To love our enemies is to decide to assist that individual in various ways to come closer to the light.

Point

To forgive is not to forget. It places any relationship on a new and more realistic plane.

WEDNESDAY — Eleventh Week of the Year
2 K 2:1, 6-14   Mt 6:1-6, 16-18

First Reading

The sweet chariot swung low, comin' for to take Elijah home. This reading describes the transfer of prophetic authority from Elijah to Elisha. Elijah splits the waters as did Moses and Joshua as a traditional sign of his role as a vehicle for God's power among the people. Elisha requests a double dose of his spirit so as to become his principal spiritual successor. After Elijah's rapture to heaven in the original "chariot of fire," a departure as abrupt as his sudden appearance, Elisha touches the waters with the prophet's cloak and they divide. The succession is intact. In Elisha, the prophetic word lives on into another age. This scene originated the legend that Elijah did not die but would return before the last days. The prophet Malachi wrote, "Before the Day of the Lord, I will send you the prophet Elijah . . ." (Ml 3:23). Jewish legends about Elijah abound. He is said to reward the good, to aid the homeless, to wander the earth in the guise of the poor, to guard newborn babies for their first 30 days. A seat is left vacant at Passover meals in case Elijah should come. Rabbis left the solution to insoluble problems in the air "until Elijah arrives." We can see, then, the importance of Elijah's presence in the Transfiguration scene.

Gospel Reading

Jesus castigates empty display. The word "hypocrite" derives from a word that originally meant "actor." The vivid illustration the Lord uses for charity is one of slipping a gift to the poor with one hand rather than ostentatiously giving a gift with both hands. If we act out our religion for all to see, we already have our applause. In our own day, His words might apply to the danger of using public piety as an evangelistic strategy, familial good example or ideological assertion while forgetting the personal depth and sincerity that make such public displays worthwhile.

Point

Elijah and Elisha were great prophets because of their intense loyalty to God. Faith, which we cannot see, is the driving force behind the public example we give which people can see.

THURSDAY — Eleventh Week of the Year
Si 48:1-14   *Mt 6:7-15*

First Reading

The Book of Sirach, written centuries after the time of Elijah and Elisha, recounts the memories of these great prophets. Elijah was the prophet of fire, a man burning with uncompromising zeal for the singlehearted service of the God of Israel. His defeat of the pagan Baal Melqart by drought and combat on Mount Carmel is the centerpiece of his memory. Finally, he was taken to heaven only to return to set things straight again before the Day of the Lord. Elisha was a wonder-working prophet, less antagonistic toward the government, whose memory is woven with miracles and legends all telling of the marvelous power of God's Word (such as the cure of Naaman the leper). The deep significance of Elijah and Elisha lies not in their personality traits but in the power of God working through them. Their stories are told to show what the Word of God can do when set free to be active in human affairs through people.

Gospel Reading

This is not necessarily the exact prayer Jesus said, although it is the way He prayed. The Lord's Prayer is less a special set of words as it is a pattern of prayer. This form of the Lord's Prayer is more frequently used by us than is Luke's version. An ancient Christian document, the *Didache*, added the phrase, "For thine is the kingdom, power and glory." That version was used by the Eastern Church and later by the Protestant churches.

The Lord tells us how to pray. We should speak to God as a Father. We should recognize His concern for our basic well-being as we submit ourselves to His providential design. Any prayer that retains these three elements is Christian prayer. Any prayer that omits them by addressing God as a remote Being or by trying to bribe Him into doing our work is not a Christian prayer.

Point

Through prayer, a deeply Trinitarian event, we allow the

*Word of God to become alive and active in and through us. It is
our umbilical cord to God.*

FRIDAY — Eleventh Week of the Year
2 K 11:1-4, 9-18, 20   *Mt 6:19-23*

First Reading

Elijah and Elisha had been prophets of the Northern kingdom of Israel. We turn our attention now to the Southern
kingdom of Judah where David's descendants continued to
rule, generally faithful to the God of their fathers. Baal Melqart
never caught on in the more conservative South. However, one
of David's descendants, Jehoroam, married a northerner,
Athaliah—a daughter of Jezebel! She brought her liberal northern ways with her and introduced the Baal cult to Jerusalem. It
was never widely popular and seemed to be limited to the elite
high government circles. When her husband and sons were
killed, Athaliah liquidated all the other royal heirs she could
find, seized the throne and proceeded to propagate the Baal
cult. Today's reading describes the fortunes of the one heir she
overlooked. Joash was sequestered until his seventh birthday
when the high priest, Jehoiada, had the army swear allegiance
to this one remaining bona fide heir of David. Athaliah was
then slain and the Baal shrines were destroyed. With this
exception, the tensions caused by Baalism in the South were
not as bloody as they were in the North. Here, the people had
never really left the worship of God.

Gospel Reading

Poor people stored their hard currency and good clothes
in the ground for a rainy day. Often, they were kept in storage
so long that they began to rot and corrode. Jesus reminds us that

our spiritual achievements, our ability to pray and believe, cannot be taken from us. We might say that just as the eye is an opening of the body which lets in both good and bad to affect us, so what guides our hearts affects the rest of our lives. How we live shows very clearly where our true loyalty lies. Whether we admit it or not, we all have a loyalty that becomes clear in the course of our lives.

Point

We show our allegiance in many more important ways than words.

SATURDAY — Eleventh Week of the Year
2 Ch 24:17-25   *Mt 6:24-34*

First Reading

The Book of Chronicles is an ecclesiastical history of Israel written for Jewish people after the exile. It sees the heart of the kingdom of David surviving in the Jerusalem Temple. As a result, it centers its story on Temple and cult. Our story continues after the young king Joash was placed in power. He had the 130 year-old Temple restored through a special tax which neither he nor the priests wanted to be blamed for collecting. Joash then invented the collection box and the Temple was eventually restored. Chronicles tells us that he was a good monarch as long as he obeyed the priests. After the high priest Jehoiada died, the elite persuaded Joash to dabble in the worship of foreign gods on the theory that a little syncretism never hurt anyone. This brought the wrath of God crashing down on Judah and Jerusalem. Joash eventually became so corrupt that he had the priest's son, the prophet Zechariah, stoned for criticizing him. Joash was punished when the Arameans captured a substantial part of his army. The adoption of pagan gods was more than disobedience. It was a surrender, in the highest circles, of national identity, internal coherence and tradition. The result was a weakness that made Judah a prey to any aggressive enemy.

Gospel Reading

Jesus' words about the flowers of the field and the birds of the air are not counsels to a careless life. We are warned against the divided loyalty of trusting God in theory while negating that in practice. The Lord invites us to a fundamental trust in God. Such a trust sees His providence continuing at work in all the events of our lives. It is the conviction that the God who gave us life will not see us disintegrate. The spiritual, loving core inside us that He fashioned and loves is safe and will thrive both in this world and in the next.

Point

Our trust in God gives us an identity, internal coherence and tradition.

MONDAY — Twelfth Week of the Year
2 K 17:5-8, 13-15, 18   *Mt 7:1-5*

First Reading

Today's first reading recounts the end of the Northern kingdom of Israel. Ripped apart by internal anarchy, Israel lost its independence to the rapidly emerging superpower of Assyria. After the king of Assyria finally invaded Israel, he deported some 27,000 of her best and brightest people and recolonized the land with foreign immigrants. With that action, the Northern kingdom of Israel was forever erased from the political map. The Second Book of Kings looks back on these tragic events and sees in them a divine judgment that flowed from the loss of the covenant's cohesive power. Israel's unity and strength were dissipated by runaway pluralism, internal discontent and the breakdown of civility. Amid all the economic and political reasons that could be adduced for Israel's collapse, the basic factor was faithlessness toward God and covenant living. This conclusion of the Book of Kings corroborated the prophetic judgments.

Gospel Reading

We do not have the perspective of hindsight from day to day. In today's Gospel reading, the Lord tells us to refrain from judging others. Of course, we all form tentative opinions on a number of issues that guide our lives. But Jesus reminds us not to close the books on any individual. God's grace is operative in every person's life at each moment and we cannot predict the result of its mysterious chemistry. Furthermore, we cannot fully comprehend the life experiences that made an individual the type of person he or she has become. Lastly, our snap judgments can be wrong. We can often mistake reticence for snobbery or anxiety for evasive behavior. As we do not want others to make harsh judgments upon us without knowing our whole story, so we should not do the same to them. There is always a story.

Point

We should be willing to give people a chance as does the Lord we follow.

TUESDAY — Twelfth Week of the Year
2 K 19:9-11, 14-21, 31-36   *Mt 7:6, 12-14*

First Reading

While the Northern kingdom of Israel was wiped off the map by Assyria, the Southern kingdom of Judah was not left unscathed. It managed to retain some tiny measure of independence as a client state of Assyria. More conservative than the North, the South was less hospitable to pagan practices and more amenable to religious reform especially after the lesson of the North's collapse. Today's reading describes a particularly memorable and dramatic occasion of deliverance as the Assyrian king Sennacherib besieged Jerusalem. King Hezekiah entered the Holy of Holies and prayed on Judah's behalf. Isaiah announced Jerusalem's deliverance as the Lord's response to Hezekiah's prayer. That night, the Assyrian army was devastated by a freak plague. This had an electric effect on the people of Judah and led to the popular belief in Jerusalem's political invulnerability. Zion was thought to be militarily impregnable. This belief will assume dangerous proportions in time as covenant living is disregarded and people rely on what was thought to be a unilateral divine promise of enduring unassailability.

Gospel Reading

We have three instructions from Jesus: to protect our religious integrity; to protect our social integrity through fair dealing with others; to protect our personal integrity whatever the difficulty. Just as the Southern kingdom of Judah followed the more difficult path of fidelity to God at the time of today's first reading and maintained strength as a people, so we are asked to recall that our strength as a Church or parish or as individuals is not a sacramental given to which the rest of our lives is irrelevant. It is the result of persistent efforts to remain faithful to the Gospel.

Point

The covenant is less a blind contract than a meeting of minds. We share God's life, love and strength to the extent that we pattern our lives on His Word.

WEDNESDAY — Twelfth Week of the Year
2 K 22:8-13; 23:1-3   Mt 7:15-20

First Reading

This incident occurred about forty years after Hezekiah's death. Because of Assyria's decline as a power, Judah had become free and independent and was in the process of religious reformation. While the Temple was being remodeled, a Book of the Torah, probably a section of what we call Deuteronomy, was discovered. This was a period of reborn nationalism and nostalgia for golden days long gone, peppered by the ominous threats of coming doom from Zephaniah and Jeremiah. Into this atmosphere of gloom and reform, the Book of Deuteronomy burst like a floodlight. King Josiah heard its words and tore his garments out of grief from the realization that Judah had been living in a fool's paradise. Through the words of Deuteronomy, Josiah and the people retrieved the ancient Mosaic covenant tradition that predated the kingly covenant tradition of David. The covenant with David had diverted attention from the more austere and bilateral Sinai covenant. Deuteronomy asserted that God's protection was not automatically assured without reciprocal and responsible covenant living. Josiah began a conservative revival. He purged magical practices, suppressed outlying shrines, and centralized all worship in Jerusalem. The Book of Deuteronomy was a prophetic impulse to return to their religious roots.

Gospel Reading

Although false prophets are present in every age, they were especially virulent in the early Church where prophets had a regular role. This warning reminds us that because something sounds religious, or claims to be sponsored by pious people, no assurance is given us that it is uplifting or spiritually enhancing. Jesus instructs us to look to the effects of a prophet's ministry or teaching in his life as well as our own. The test of teaching is practice. We should examine whether a prophet's words make our lives more spiritually unified, give us peace, and draw us closer to the Church community Jesus founded. We should test whether a particular prophetic message facilitates our prayer, allows us to see God's will in our lives more clearly, generates deeper harmony among a wide variety of people and makes the Gospel words come to special life for us.

Point

Prophets can hold us back or lead us forward. All are to be tested by their own lives and the unity they bring to our own.

THURSDAY — Twelfth Week of the Year
2 K 24:8-17   Mt 7:21-29

First Reading

This is the first scene of the last act of the Southern kingdom of Judah. Jehoiachin was the son of a particularly corrupt and tyrannical king who had been condemned by Jeremiah.

Because the circumstances of the reformer Josiah's death in battle ten years earlier seemed to indicate divine repudiation of his conservative reform, it was put on the shelf. Now the sins of his father are visited on Jehoiachin. Assyria is gone from the picture as Babylon rises to the ascendant position. This reading depicts an initial deportation of Judah's elite into exile with a puppet king left in charge. Jeremiah's forecast of impending doom was coming true.

Gospel Reading

At the end of the Sermon on the Mount, Jesus rejects the outward display of religiosity as a guarantee of divine help. To speak of a Christian nation or a people of faith implies a great deal more than the insignia of religion, prayer in schools, chaplains in legislatures, religious mottoes, hymns at inaugurations and prayerful invocations at public dinners. More crucially, it is putting the Lord's teachings into practice. It is the effort to achieve some measure of justice in domestic policy and morality in foreign policy. The same is true of a family. To be a Christian family is more than church attendance. It is discipleship on a daily basis. The Sermon began with the Beatitudes which grounded true discipleship. It ends with the warning that the practical implementation of these attitudes is the safeguard against a temporary spiritual enthusiasm and is the foundation of a mature and effective spirituality.

Point

To be long-lived, faith and reform must be more than skin deep. They must reach heart, mind and life style.

FRIDAY — Twelfth Week of the Year
2 K 25:1-12

Mt 8:1-4

First Reading

This reading describes the devastation of Jerusalem. Zedekiah was a weak king for several reasons. Since the legitimate ruler, Jehoiachin, was still in exile, Zedekiah's leverage over the remaining inhabitants of Jerusalem was minimal. Zealots, meanwhile, were planning a revolt against Babylon. Jeremiah saw such rebellion as political suicide and counseled against it. After some mugwumping, Zedekiah finally sided with the revolutionaries. The insurgency took place and caused the king of Babylon to put Jerusalem under siege. The result was disaster. The city was destroyed and most of the remaining population deported. The exile is an historical watershed which will prove to be a political and spiritual catharsis for Judah. Her days of political glory are gone forever as she prepares now for a new spiritual role on the world scene.

Gospel Reading

After the Sermon on the Mount, Jesus continues His ministry with a set of ten miracles showing His concrete fulfillment of the Old Testament promises and pointing the way for the Church's ministry. Jesus' healing of a leper is more than another miracle. It signifies the healing of the outcast, the downtrodden and the exile. Lepers were all of these. They were cast out and exiled from their own people and were virtually penniless. Through this healed leper, Jesus extends His love to all those who are burdened by a suffering which no one cares to alleviate. Even to those minorities which our mainstream society and churches refuse to touch, Jesus is present. When we care for them, the miracle of healing recurs—theirs and ours.

Point

Even when the Temple was gone, God remained among His people to remind them that He is with them in a deeper way.

SATURDAY — Twelfth Week of the Year
Lm 2:2, 10-14, 18-19   Mt 8:5-17

First Reading

The Book of Lamentations was written at the beginning of the exile, while the wound was still fresh. It describes the condition of Judah and her exiles in five poems of overwhelming grief and sorrow. In a way that no narrative history can convey, it captures the disorientation, the bitterness and the questioning of God as to the reason for this turn of events. Everything that Jerusalem and Judah represented seemed to be forever destroyed. Yet, in the middle of this despair is a firm faith that God lives. It is a national version of Job's lament. It affirms that the destruction of Jerusalem was not an irrational absurdity but part of God's judgment. God was dealing with shallow fidelity, facile theology and religious myopia. In the middle of its grief, Lamentations summons up the faith to say, as did Job, "I know that my Redeemer lives." Providence was present even in national suffering. This angle of vision explains the use of Lamentations in the Good Friday liturgy.

Gospel Reading

Jesus heals the centurion's servant and Peter's mother-in-law. Matthew interprets these healings with a reference to Isaiah. Jesus not only fulfilled the prophecy of a healing Messiah; He was also that mysterious Suffering Servant of Isaiah who, in some enigmatic way, absorbed the pain of mankind to render it redemptive. Jesus identified Himself with mankind so intimately and profoundly that the pain of every person became part of Him. He took away the crushing mortality of suffering and endowed it with the power to save.

Point

Through faith, suffering can be transformative.

MONDAY — Thirteenth Week of the Year
Am 2:6-10, 13-16 *Mt 8:18-22*

First Reading

For the next two weeks, the prophecies of Amos and Hosea will reveal an inside view of the spiritual and political corruption that pervaded the Northern kingdom of Israel prior to its collapse. Amos was a southerner who traveled to the North and prophesied there during a time of unusual economic prosperity and corruption. He denounces these excesses in today's first reading. The peasants who had formed the backbone of the nation were now being exploited by the new rich as small land holdings were gobbled up by huge estates. He vividly portrays the greed of the wealthy as they oppress the poor and quite literally take the shirts off their backs as collateral for usurious loans. He is exposing a cancerous social structure built upon a temporary flush of post-war prosperity, and he calls Israel back to her ancient tribal tradition of community responsibility—all to no avail. Without covenant living, the very affluence that seemed such a blessing was really a handicap in disguise.

Gospel Reading

Jesus warns those who wish to follow Him that they should be prepared to live simply, be attached to nothing and to allow nothing to delay or hinder their discipleship. All of this is applicable on a deeper level. It would be too facile to expect the simple elimination of material goods to release a Niagara of spiritual insight. In fact, voluntary poverty can well be a way of evading community responsibility. Even in a monastery or convent it is difficult to follow Christ. The temptations there are more subtle and it may even be necessary to work with greater effort to keep faith because the liturgy and words of Scripture can easily become too familiar and lose their drama, power and bite. Wealth is not the only obstacle to following the Lord. We all have to do some dying inside to let the risen Lord come to life within us. There is no escaping that.

Point

There is no automatic entry to spiritual vitality without the hard challenge of community covenant living.

TUESDAY — Thirteenth Week of the Year
Am 3:1-8; 4:11-12   *Mt 8:23-27*

First Reading

This reading is the heart of Amos' prophetic message about the covenant. The conventional wisdom was that Israel's special calling as God's people assured prosperity and prestige. Amos reverses that implication. Precisely because the people of Israel are God's chosen people, they are held to a higher standard of conduct. Just as we expect a greater sensitivity toward us from people we know well, so God expected a higher standard from the people to whom He had revealed Himself and whom He had blessed. This was a time of Israel's political expansion. Amos is very much a dissident prophet here in his announcement that the punishment of God's chosen people will be greater than that meted out to others. To show that God is in control of events, Amos asks a series of "Is the Pope Catholic?" questions and concludes with his central affirmation that if evil falls upon Israel, it will not be by accident but by the Lord's judgment. To the superficial faith of the people that saw the Day of the Lord as a golden future of prosperity, Amos asserts that it will instead be one of devastatingly honest accounting.

Gospel Reading

The storm on the lake showed the fragility of the disciples' faith. The expression of Jesus' power in bringing calm not only revealed His majesty but the utter dependence of the disciples in any age to find their source of peace in the Lord alone. As was the case with Israel, we who have been called by and know the Lord are held to a higher standard than others. We are expected to have greater faith and trust in Him especially during difficult times that beset us all. Through us the Lord can bring His peace to others.

Point

A greater responsibility attaches to those who have been gifted with faith.

WEDNESDAY — Thirteenth Week of the Year
Am 5:14-15, 21-24   Mt 8:28-34

First Reading

In today's first reading, Amos describes the religious face

of Israel's internal decay. Popular attendance at the local shrines was never bigger. It was, however, ritual with a heavy pagan overlay from decades of religion-shopping that had been going on in the North. More deeply, life and worship lost their connection. Ritual observance was lip-service alone. A splendid liturgy obscured a society that was sick to death. Amos asserts that the responsibilities that go along with being a covenant people are not discharged through ceremonies alone. Sabbath observance was only one of many commandments. The obligations of the covenant were to be fulfilled in justice and social concern as well. As long as these deeper covenantal obligations were neglected, the liturgical festivals with all of their elaborate liturgies were simply ritual eyewash.

Gospel Reading

After this remarkable exorcism, the people begged Jesus to leave the neighborhood. They might have been frightened by the religious fireworks. More probably, they saw the Lord as a threat to the status quo. The same can be true of our spiritual lives. It is much easier to settle for the outward forms of religion than to let the Spirit enter deep inside us where He might unsettle the attitudes, work habits and relationships with our neighbors to which we have become accustomed over the years. Because such radical self-examination is often portrayed as fanatical and dangerous, it is much easier to settle for a set of tame and predictable religious observances. Jesus calls us to much more than that.

Point

Prayer is not like a Buddhist prayer wheel that turns independently of the rest of our lives. Prayer that God hears comes not simply from our lips but emerges from how we live.

THURSDAY — Thirteenth Week of the Year
Am 7:10-17   *Mt 9:1-8*

First Reading

Amos was not a professional prophet. There were bands of full time prophets who, by this time, had sold themselves into government service in the North and thereby lost their capacity to criticize existing policies. In this reading, Amos comes into conflict with one of them. Amaziah reports to Jeroboam II, the northern king, that Amos was going public with his predictions of doom and judgment on the kingdom during a time of political prosperity. With the king's permission, Amaziah tells Amos that his prophecies are not welcome in the North and that he should return to the South where they will pay him handsomely for such doomsaying over the North. Amos responds that he is not a professional prophet but a gardener who was commissioned directly by God to warn the political and religious establishments of the impending judgment. He concludes with an especially severe judgment not only against the North but against Amaziah in particular.

Gospel Reading

There is conflict as well between Jesus and the religious establishment which has much more to do with conflicting visions of faith and God than with the forgiveness of sin. As so often happens in the Gospels, what seem to be conflicts over single issues actually bring to the surface far larger differences between Jesus and the religious professionals of His day. In this sense, Jesus was a prophet like Amos, calling the Church of His time back to the vitality of its traditional heritage. Like Amos, Jesus was not welcome. Churches can often be more deaf to the prophetic word than is the world. A perfectionism and herd instinct in things religious can cause people of faith to disregard minorities among them who often represent neglected values. People who are different are unfortunately treated as disloyal.

Point

Prophets are sent by God from within the Church not only to the world but to the Church itself.

FRIDAY — Thirteenth Week of the Year
Am 8:4-6, 9-12   *Mt 9:9-13*

First Reading

Today's first reading gives us another look at the glittery exterior of popular religion in Israel during the time of Amos. He describes the wealthy people's perfunctory religious observances as they await the conclusion of the Sabbath so they can resume overcharging the poor and weighting the scales. Their minds were not on the holy day but on the next day's profits. Amos pronounces the judgment of God that they will be left in their indifference. There will be a famine of the Word of God in the land. No one will be called forth to point out wrongdoing. They will be left alone on the slippery slope. This is a profound punishment because it removes a society's opportunity for self-correction. We can imagine the state of our society if we had never had any environmentalists among us, if no civil rights advocates had ever existed, if peace activists had never spoken a word. Our society would be plagued by undrinkable water and unbreathable air, living at the point of dangerous racial explosions, transformed into an armed camp. Prophets are important.

Gospel Reading

In this reading, Jesus reminds us that He came for sinners.

He came for those who know they have done wrong and seek reconciliation. There is a world of difference between the wrongdoer who has lost any capacity to distinguish between right and wrong in his life and the person who realizes that he has sinned and now seeks the power to begin a different course. The case of Matthew exhibits an incident of the latter. It reminds us of the great gift of conscience and, for the baptized, of the Holy Spirit within us—and for Catholics, of the Church's teaching. These are factors we can summon forth to help us renew and change our lives no matter what we have done in the past. We can contrast this with the case of an individual whose life is seriously and morally dysfunctional, but who is not even aware of that fact. Such a person lives unaware of the cancer rotting inside until it is too late.

Point

We all fall short of the glory of God. Realizing that truth is the beginning of growth in our spiritual life.

SATURDAY — Thirteenth Week of the Year
Am 9:11-15
                                                      Mt 9:14-17

First Reading

The prophecy of Amos concludes with a word of hope. Even though his message is one of impending doom, his vision pierces beyond the coming darkness to a time of light and restoration. Amos speaks in metaphors of a restoration, but not of the economic and political power of Israel. That is gone. He speaks instead of a resurgence of her spiritual power as a rejuvenated people of God. He points to a day when they will be united not by blood, soil or cult but by fidelity to God. The doom Amos predicted came a generation later. The restoration he envisioned arrived six centuries after on a hill in the South called Calvary.

Gospel Reading

The Lord speaks of new wine in new skins. The wine and bread are connecting links of the new people of God formed in Jesus. Jesus revived the ancient Mosaic tradition of a covenant people. He linked His disciples together by ties deeper than those of soil, blood and Law. It was on a level of faith and spirit that men and women of every culture and nation would be able to share in the richness and blessings that Amos foresaw. What stands in the way of this new international spiritual community is sin. The Lord has entrusted to us the means to eradicate that basic barrier. We hold in the sacraments the means for the renewal not only of a parish, nation or Church but of the entire human race.

Point

The renewal of spiritual community among people is possible through the body and blood of Jesus.

MONDAY — Fourteenth Week of the Year
Ho 2:16-18, 21-22   Mt 9:18-26

First Reading

Hosea was a native prophet through whom we have another insight into the spiritual decay that destroyed the Northern kingdom of Israel. His perspective is more optimistic than that of Amos. Spiritual insight can emerge from many situations. In Hosea's case, it was a wife who left him to become, or return to being, a lady of the evening (and morning and noon . . .). "She had a ring on her finger, but time on her hands." In his own continuing love despite her infidelity,

Hosea saw a parable of God's love for Israel. In this first reading, Hosea sees Israel's adoption and tolerance of pagan religious practices as a form of cultural and spiritual adultery. The Lord speaks through Hosea of a second honeymoon when He will take the unfaithful Israel back to the desert (the exile) and there renew the marriage bond—their covenant. As Amos spoke of the certainty and power of God's judgment, Hosea describes the healing power of God's abiding love for us even in our sins.

Gospel Reading

One message that speaks out very clearly from this double miracle is that if we are to be healed, we must reach out to God. We have to be at least willing to touch the bottom of Jesus' garment. It is not psychologically or emotionally possible for us to completely abandon our old ways overnight. But if we make the slightest movement in the Lord's direction He will extend His hand to us, grasp our hand through His grace, and lift us up to complete what we have begun. If we make that initial gesture, the Lord's healing power will rush out upon us. First, however, we have to reach out to Him.

Point

The fidelity to and intimacy with God that we all once knew is never forever lost as long as we have enough life to reach toward the Lord.

TUESDAY — Fourteenth Week of the Year
Ho 8:4-7, 11-13   Mt 9:32-38

First Reading

Hosea is alluding to the political chaos that followed the death of Jeroboam II under whom Israel had known prosperity and stability. After his death, the internal fissures that Amos denounced cracked wide open. Within the ensuing decade, there were five kings, three coups and several assassinations. Darkening this internal anarchy was the encroaching and aggressively militant Assyria. Israel's political instability resulted in policy confusion, the collapse of law and order and the seizure of power without any pretense of legitimacy. Unlike the Southern kingdom of Judah which maintained a single Davidic dynasty until its end, Israel was jerked back and forth by intramural dissent. Pervading all this was the rampant paganism of the Baal cult. Hosea identifies Israel's fundamental problem as a religious one. The natural consequences of her spiritual infidelity will have a multiplier effect. It will send shock waves through her families, neighborhoods and political life. He phrases it as, "sowing the wind and reaping a whirlwind." Israel looked to the wrong things for strength.

Gospel Reading

The crowds which followed Jesus found something in Him which their teachers were unable to give. They were grasping for a word of truth or comfort. We see a similar phenomenon today. People are seeking various ways to know God in a fashion that will pull together the different parts of their lives. They seek a bedrock upon which they can rely. Self-help books and popular psychology books that fill the supermarket racks can give temporary relief; but they testify to the nearly universal search for healing. The trendy cure of one year is forgotten in the next. If we place our trust in the temporary and superficial, as did Israel, that misplaced faith will come back to haunt us. Healthy human living is a function of our communion with God. That is the message of the Book of Genesis. When that communion is cut off, the situation is similar to a house designed to be built on rock having been constructed on sand. The owner spends the rest of his life and money finding temporary buttresses and supports to hold up a structure that is intrinsically insecure.

Point

If we seek comfort from illusions, we will find illusory comfort. The strength that comes from God cannot be found in things.

WEDNESDAY — Fourteenth Week of the Year
Ho 10:1-3, 7-8, 12   *Mt 10:1-7*

First Reading

Hosea excoriates the gross affluence of Israel's sin. The more abundant their fruit, the more altars they built to the pagan gods. The more profit Israel made, the more it spent on its infidelity. He is describing the evils of a flourishing society. The emotional hook that makes Hosea's description so graphic is the wrenching personal experience of his own wife's infidelity—a model of Israel's departure from God. Hosea speaks of a time of justice when God will rain down judgment on Israel for its wild and wanton ways. It is easy to caricature the Old Testament prophets as killjoys intent on sucking the fun out of living. We should recall that their condemnation of idolatry was more than an unenlightened anti-ecumenical tirade. The worship of the Baals had social and attitudinal consequences. The pagan emphasis on fertility (as does sexual aggressivity in our own day) corroded the marriage bond and personal and family loyalty as well as faithfulness to the God of Israel.

Gospel Reading

After the long Sermon on the Mount and a review of Jesus'

ministry to paralytics, outcasts and the unclean, Matthew now
shows Him telling His disciples to hit the trail and preach. For
each person, there comes a similar moment. We celebrate the
Eucharist and experience a spiritual lift; then comes a moment
when we have to leave the church building and take our faith
into our world. There we meet frustrations, sickness, affluence
and love. As with Hosea's strained marriage, such experiences
can challenge our faith. They can also clarify and deepen it.
Our life experiences can enable us to attain a deeper insight
into the workings of God. The more diverse our experience, the
more material is available for our insight.

Point

*Wherever we travel, geographically or emotionally, God
can always be found.*

THURSDAY — Fourteenth Week of the Year
Ho 11:3-4, 8-9   *Mt 10:7-15*

First Reading

This reading from Hosea is one of the richest passages for
prayer in the Old Testament. It is a story of God's love, human
refusal, divine discipline and restoration. It is really the story of
every human being's pilgrimage to God. Just as each of us can
tell our own personal story, so we have our own personal
covenant with the Lord. No two are alike. It may be stormy and
turbulent as was Israel's or quiet and trusting as was Mary's.
There are times when we fail and think that we have lost the
Lord's love forever. God reminds us through Hosea that He is
God and not a human being who carries grudges. With God we
can always go home again. When the Lord forgives us, we are
forgiven forever.

Gospel Reading

Jesus tells His disciples to travel light. If their attention is on the Gospel message, everything else will fall into place. The Church's great message of reconciliation and forgiveness is our good news to a troubled, mistrusting and angry world. When we describe divine forgiveness, we move beyond the human models of armistices, peace treaties, and reparations to the model of Jesus Christ. He is the model of a loving and free forgiveness that heals and makes whole.

Point

For many people bound by guilt, the question is not whether God will forgive but whether they are willing to forgive themselves by accepting His gift of reconciliation. We can come home again.

FRIDAY — Fourteenth Week of the Year
Ho 14:2-10   *Mt 10:16-23*

First Reading

In reading the Bible, we should remember that behind each of its books is a story and a distinctively human experience through which God speaks to us. In this reading, He speaks of a relationship restored. We all have had the experience of loving someone only to have that individual hurt or betray us as Gomer did Hosea. Hosea went a step further than most of us to see in that wrenching, personal wounding an image of sin. In the face of her infidelity, Hosea knew that he still loved Gomer. He would not give up. Many of us may have had a similar reaction. Again, Hosea went a step further than most of us to see in his love for Gomer a suggestion of what

God's love for us is like. If we have experienced unreciprocated
love, we have a deeper insight into sin and grace than is
available in any theology book.

Gospel Reading

Jesus discusses the problems of persecution and of the
betrayal even of those who preach His word. These problems
will plague Christian disciples until the end of time. A conclusion we can draw from our week with Hosea in the light of this
missionary instruction from the Lord is a stark one. Unlike the
popular image of love as romantic and carefree, the truth is that
love hurts. It can be very painful. It is sacrificial. Yet, it can
transform, heal and enlarge a person. It is not an exclusive
possession of the young. Love is more than warm puppy dogs,
meadows in the Spring, or long walks on moonlit nights. It is an
adult project. For all its power, love hurts.

Point

*The most realistic symbol of love is not a cupid but a cross.
On the cross, human love and divine love intersect. In the
sacrifice of the cross, humanity and God are linked together in
love.*

SATURDAY — Fourteenth Week of the Year
Is 6:1-8   *Mt 10:24-33*

First Reading

We turn our attention now to one of the great prophets of
the Southern kingdom of Judah. If Hosea spoke of the intimate

love of God, Isaiah of Jerusalem is the herald of the sovereign majesty of God at work in the power politics of his time. Isaiah loved Jerusalem and the dynasty of David. He prophesied for about a half-century during the time of Judah's decline. After the death of the popular and astute king Uzziah, a deepening sense of crisis and doom fell across the land from the direction of Assyria. In the rapid flux of political events Isaiah saw not only political danger but a spiritual emergency as well. In today's first reading, we have the scene of his prophetic call. During a temple liturgy, he had an overwhelming vision of God's glory. In this powerful vision, he realized that although Uzziah was dead and Assyria threatened, God is still the ultimate King. His glory is not lodged in a remote heaven but fills the earth if one has the sight to see it. This vision launched Isaiah's prophetic career with a sense of his own and the people's collective unworthiness of this pervasive, all-holy presence of God. Isaiah is sent to speak of the coming purification and cleansing.

Gospel Reading

Jesus speaks of the real danger that faces us as being much more disastrous than physical harm. Spiritual crisis can be fatal because it can erode whatever source of hope we might have to repair our lives. The real threat to our fundamental well-being is a person who can rob us of our faith, our hope and our capacity to love others. Skepticism, cynicism and agnosticism can be more fatal than any physical danger.

Point

In the middle of our political or economic difficulties, the greatest danger and greatest hope remain spiritual ones.

MONDAY — Fifteenth Week of the Year
Is 1:10-17   *Mt 10:34-11:1*

First Reading

Judah's transition from a tribal to an urban culture caused less dislocation of the social structure than it did in Israel. Nevertheless, there was injustice and exploitation in the South. This is the subject of the oracle from Isaiah's early years in today's first reading. He characterizes the sinfulness of Judah's conduct by evoking the names of Sodom and Gomorrah, household synonyms for corruption. The injustice among the people was a fissure that would eventually cause the social structure of Judah to crumble. Isaiah says in effect that if our life is corrupt, our prayer is corrupt. If our lives as covenant people are lies, our rituals are lies. Isaiah does not call for liturgical reformation. The liturgy was dutifully observed and ceremonially august. He points, rather, to the social and economic gaps between rich and poor that were slowly and insidiously poisoning Judah as they had Israel.

Gospel Reading

Jesus makes a related point in today's Gospel reading. He ends the missionary sermon by speaking of the complete dedication required of a disciple in very severe terms. The language is strong and total. Just as prayer is not a separate track but an expression of our lives, so "dedication" is not a certain thing or set of "things" we do but a way of doing everything else. Dedication is functionally an adjective rather than a noun. Our spiritual life, then, is not simply a collection of isolated prayerful moments in our daily schedule. It is a way of living.

Point

We must take care not to let our spiritual life and our "real life" drift apart. Keeping them together is the mark of an adult and practiced Christian.

TUESDAY — Fifteenth Week of the Year
Is 7:1-9   *Mt 11:20-24*

First Reading

This reading is the stage setting for the famous Immanuel prophecy of Isaiah. High politics are rampant in this scene from the second phase of Isaiah's prophetic career. At this time, Assyria was gaining enormous power. The king of Israel and the king of Aram (Syria) sought to force Judah's Ahaz to join their anti-Assyrian alliance—or else! Ahaz has the choice of becoming a puppet of Israel and Aram or of Assyria. He is between the proverbial rock and a hard place. He is told through Isaiah to stand firm and to avoid any pro- or anti-Assyrian alliances. Isaiah tells him to stand on the promises God made to David. Any kind of alliance would be political suicide. As Ahaz wavers, Isaiah tells him to ask for a sign that God's promise to David is real. Ahaz refuses with some patronizing cant. Isaiah responds that the sign will be the birth of an heir—and that before he reaches the age of reason, the anti-Assyrian alliance would break up. Ahaz sided with Assyria and eventually paid a price. Isaiah repeatedly called for social reform which Ahaz refused to implement. Instead he put his trust in the less demanding route of facile alliances.

Gospel Reading

Jesus reproaches the towns that refused to believe His signs. There is a special meaning to the word "sign." In its classic biblical sense, it is more than a miracle; it is the Word of God made visible. It is in this sense that Isaiah could speak of

God's promise of an enduring dynasty coming true through a baby's birth. In this same sense as well, Jesus' healings and exorcisms were manifestations of His healing and liberating word. These were the signs that the towns around Capernaum refused to credit. It is not just individuals but organized entities that can become faithless. Refusal of the Lord's word can bring collective as well as individual judgment.

Point

The signs of God's love and judgment can be present in political and economic events as well as in ecclesiastical ones. They are found not only in supernatural events but also in how natural events come together.

WEDNESDAY — Fifteenth Week of the Year
Is 10:5-7, 13-16   Mt 11:25-27

First Reading

In a striking assertion of divine sovereignty over the course of history, Isaiah states that God is using the superpower of Assyria to work His will. This is an important component of Isaiah's theology. God is at work among the nations, to achieve His purposes. Eventually, Assyria herself will receive judgment. At this point, however, she was an unconscious instrument of divine reprisal and cleansing. There is a deep divine design running through history. It is very speculative for us to interpret every political or economic event as God's affirmative will because we seldom can see the full scope, range and direction of the consequences of immediate historical events. Not every diagnosis of cancer or economic downturn is a sign of God's judgment. It requires the gift of prophetic insight to interpret the welter of events around us in the light of the Holy

Spirit. The fact that prophecy is a gift implies that we are not all prophets.

Gospel Reading

The revelation of God's will is not necessarily a function of theological understanding. Jesus tells us that a revelation can be given to the merest children—that is, to ordinary people. If economic prosperity were an infallible sign of God's blessing and recession an equally clear sign of punishment, there would be no need for the gifts of revelation or prophecy. The interpretation of history would be very mechanical. It is precisely because we do not have a wide enough screen on which to view events (both in our own lives as well as those of history) that we see discernment as a gift. God's will is indeed operative in secular history as well as in our individual lives. Discerning that will is not a function of a person's IQ but of spiritual insight.

Point

Spiritual insight is born in prayer and not in school.

THURSDAY — Fifteenth Week of the Year
Is 26:7-9, 12, 16-19   *Mt 11:28-30*

First Reading

Isaiah speaks of revival. The events that befell Judah in these years could well have destroyed her faith. Hope and faith survived in large part because of Isaiah. Over the years, the Sinai covenant with its call for responsible community behavior became overlaid with the theology of the Davidic covenant. This latter was interpreted as an unconditional promise of invulnerability irrespective of the moral behavior of king or nation. The Assyrian crisis caused such an optimistic theology to collapse. Isaiah reinterpreted the Davidic covenant as a firm promise with the possibility of chastisement. God would show enough love for His people to pull them back from the brink by allowing a remnant to survive. Further, Isaiah gradually taught the people to look beyond the existing political entity to a larger and more enduring dynasty and kingdom. The Immanuel sign given to Ahaz was only part of this larger theme of Messianism in Isaiah. This is one reason why the entire book of Isaiah is popular liturgical reading during Advent. In today's reading, Isaiah describes the chastisement of Judah as analogous to a woman giving birth to a new and strong spiritual community. This is the first Old Testament reference to resurrection—a brand new and inspired category that bursts open the existing horizon to a future into which prophetic hopes would now be poured.

Gospel Reading

The invitation of Jesus to the weary and burdened is the fulfillment of Isaiah's prophecy. He has carried the eternal burden of our sins. He has been chastised in our place. In Him, there is always available to us a place of light and refreshment where we can unload our sins and be given new life. He embodies the new Israel to whom all the promises of Isaiah came true.

Point

The fulfillment the Lord brings is primarily spiritual, from which all other kinds of success and fulfillment are derivative.

FRIDAY — Fifteenth Week of the Year
Is 38:1-6, 21-22, 7-8   Mt 12:1-8

First Reading

Hezekiah's illness and recovery are also a parable about

Judah. The word of the Lord comes to him through the prophet Isaiah warning of impending death. When Hezekiah (son of Ahaz) repents, God promises to deliver him from the king of Assyria. In fact, this is a miniature version of what occurred when Assyrian armies approached Jerusalem. Hezekiah prayed in Solomon's Temple and Jerusalem was saved after a plague struck the enemy army. The message of these stories is one of divine forgiveness and not of divine vengeance. To those who repent, God is willing to open an avenue of salvation and restoration. The line of kings who ruled over Judah were, after David's death, a disappointing lot. Their defects led Isaiah to point to a time when a Messianic king would come who would be God's unique agent to bring out the best in Judah and her individual inhabitants.

Gospel Reading

In another one of the nagging controversies that the Pharisees initiated throughout Jesus' public career, the Lord asserts the forgiving nature of the Father rather than His vengeance. There is something deep, almost genetic, in human nature that insists on viewing God as a God of reprisals and revenge. What was difficult for Jesus to convey was that God is a Father, a God of forgiveness and love. Perhaps we too easily project our own urge to retaliate onto God. It is extremely difficult for most of us to genuinely appreciate the total, profound and cleansing nature of God's love once we accept it.

Point

We should try to model our forgiveness of others on God's forgiveness of us rather than vice versa.

SATURDAY — Fifteenth Week of the Year
Mi 2:1-5   Mt 12:14-21

First Reading

The prophet Micah was a native of Judah and a contemporary of Isaiah during Hezekiah's reign. Two prophets could not be more different. If Isaiah was urban and urbane and involved in things of the Temple, Micah was very much the rustic man of the land somewhat anti-urban in his view of Jerusalem and Samaria as the seats of corruption. The evil that Micah condemns, however, is the same as that pointed out by Isaiah. Micah speaks of the injustices which landholders suffered at the hands of their landlords. He had witnessed the Assyrian devastation of the North and now anticipates the coming threat to the South as a judgment of God. The very lands that these landlords coveted would be taken from them as they became the laughingstock of others. Micah was the first Old Testament prophet to predict the destruction of Jerusalem.

Gospel Reading

Today's Gospel reading suggests the different approaches that Jesus used in His ministry. Matthew quotes Isaiah to show that Jesus also will proclaim justice not by crying out words of condemnation but more subtly, by putting His message into practice. We see a contrast here in prophetic styles. There are different ways of living the Gospel: some do so in a way that is dramatically public. Others do so in a way that is less so. It is important that the Gospel message be preached and brought to bear on people's hearts. It is not necessary that any particular individual receive the credit for doing so.

Point

Each of us eventually finds his or her own way to live out

God's Word. There is no single Christian style. The Spirit will use our individual and sometimes idiosyncratic personalities.

MONDAY — Sixteenth Week of the Year
Mi 6:1-4, 6-8   *Mt 12:38-42*

First Reading

This is the high point of Micah's prophecy. He pictures a kind of trial with the mountains and hills sitting in the jury box. Judah is the defendant. The Lord is the plaintiff-prosecutor. He rehearses what He has done on Judah's behalf in the Exodus and through the leadership of Moses. He recalls the special covenant made with Judah. Then Judah responds in effect: "We have sinned. How can we make reparation? Tons of sacrifices? Thousands of rams and rivers of oil? The sacrifice of our firstborn? Point out the length, style and richness of the liturgy you want to make amends." The Lord answers that He does not want more liturgy. The issue is not a ritual one. He replies that Judah should only do what is right, love goodness and walk humbly before her God. This succinct trinity summarizes the messages of Amos, Hosea and Isaiah. It is the heart of eighth century prophecy and of prophecy in any age.

Gospel Reading

Jesus is asked to present signs to establish His credentials. He refuses: the great sign will be the Resurrection. He remarks that there is no need for spectacular signs to prove the validity of His words. He recalls the repentance of pagans without signs at the words of Jonah. The search of the Queen of the South for Solomon's wisdom also reflected an authentic quest for truth and not for magic signs. Here, the Lord is explaining the heart of the Torah Law while the Pharisees insist on a miracle as though that sign alone and not the content of His teaching were the ultimate test of credibility. Their problem is much deeper than puzzlement over Jesus' identity. If an individual is unwilling to hear God's word, a thousand miracles will not suffice. If we are willing to listen, we will find plenty of signs of His presence.

Point

To walk humbly before our God is the precondition for hearing His Word.

TUESDAY — Sixteenth Week of the Year
Mi 7:14-15, 18-20   *Mt 12:46-50*

First Reading

This first reading is taken from the end of Micah's prophecy. It is a liturgical prayer for restoration. Micah came from the land and many of the images he uses lose a great deal of their evocative power when we are away from natural symbols. Bashan and Gilead were extremely fertile regions that Israel had once possessed. He looks forward to a time of restoration. For those of us who live in an urban culture, these nature symbols represent restoration, healing and forgiveness.

Gospel Reading

Jesus tells us that the bond between people in the new covenant is not one of blood as with the Jews but one of faith. Blood is not necessarily thicker than water. Frequently, we feel a closer attachment to our friends than we do to our family members. Jesus reminds us that the real link with God is not from blood, geography, or ethnic origin but from hearing God's word and keeping it. The promise of restoration (the gift of personal peace) is given to those who hear and try to keep God's word. This cannot be reduced to slogans or to an itemized list of specific religious practices. It describes a way of living. To do right, to love goodness and to walk humbly before God together compose the gift of personal peace.

Point

"Any who did accept Him He empowered to become children of God. These are they who believe in His name — who were begotten not by blood, nor by carnal desire nor by man's willing it, but by God" (Jn 1:12-13).

WEDNESDAY — Sixteenth Week of the Year
Jr 1:1, 4-10   *Jt 13:1-9*

First Reading

Jeremiah was a southern prophet whose ministry spanned a time of religious reformation in Judah together with a repudiation of that revival followed by the eventual collapse of the South, the devastation of Jerusalem and exile. He was from a priestly family whose roots were located in the traditional shrine at Shiloh. Today's first reading describes Jeremiah's call as a young man. God selects him from his very beginnings to speak not only words of judgment, destruction and suffering but also words of hope, eventual restoration and revival. Jeremiah lived in a time of apostasy and idolatry. He identified himself very closely with the sins of his people. In this reading, God calls him from among a sinful people to make him a special instrument of the divine Word in his time. There is no school for prophecy. Prophets are made so by God, often unwillingly.

Gospel Reading

Jesus tells the beloved parable of the sown seed that fell in all sorts of places. Much like the prophetic word that strikes people differently, the Gospel message is greeted with indifference, brief enthusiasm and shallow excitement—and also with faith. It is this last category that produces a spectacular harvest not only in the lives of those who believe but in their ability to bring that word to others.

Point

However packaged by the personality and style of the prophet, the word of God has power precisely because it is from God.

THURSDAY — Sixteenth Week of the Year
Jr 2:1-3, 7-8, 12-13   *Mt 13:10-17*

First Reading

Jeremiah evokes an image we did not find in Isaiah. He speaks of the Exodus and the ancient covenant with Moses. This was the time of the great and sweeping effort called the Deuteronomic reform under King Josiah. A section of the Book we call Deuteronomy was discovered in the Temple and a massive effort was initiated to return to the old Mosaic covenant that preceded the popularized theology of the Davidic covenant. Jeremiah describes the honeymoon of Israel (and Judah) with God in the wilderness. He speaks of the affluence of the promised land and the later infidelities with pagan idols. In place of living water, they have dug wells with their own hands—wells that are unable to save or give life. Human fabrications of religiosity could not replace the worship of the God who gives life.

Gospel Reading

Jesus used parables to present the message of God's life and dominion from a new angle. The direct message could easily fall on deaf ears. So often we become attuned to buzz words and familiar categories that soothe and no longer puncture our conscience and awareness. The Lord's parables were direct images that presented a profound truth in an imaginative and unexpected way to ambush our complacency. If an individual had really blinded himself to the truth, the parables became opaque and hid the message of the kingdom.

Point

Jeremiah's dramatics and Jesus' parables were both ways of bringing a saving word to people who had become anesthetized to saving truth.

FRIDAY — Sixteenth Week of the Year
Jr 3:14-17   *Mt 13:18-23*

First Reading

The Book of Jeremiah is an anthology of oracles which he delivered at various times during a long and distracted forty year period that saw swift international and national political shifts. This oracle speaks of a return after Jerusalem had already been destroyed. Jeremiah foresees a revival of the ancient faith centered in Jerusalem. It will be spearheaded by the faithful few who hear God's word and keep it. Jerusalem has been an image of the renewed Church in every age. God works through minorities to renew the whole. Jeremiah looks to a time when they will no longer need the ark of the covenant. This is a fierce way of saying that religion will pervade the whole of life. At this point, religion had no spillover into the everyday lives of the people. Jeremiah looks beyond these days to a time when the line between sacred and secular will be erased and all of life will be an act of worship. This complete penetration of religion and life took place in Jesus Christ.

Gospel Reading

Lack of penetration is the subject of today's Gospel reading. This interpretation of the Lord's parable is one which the early Church cherished and preserved. This anatomy of the types of response to the Gospel is still true. Various applications can be made. We can consider the viewpoint of the homilist. The seed along the path that hears without listening are those for whom the beginning of a homily is the signal to tune out, sink into reverie or doze. These people have concluded a priori that sermons are a useless interlude. The seed on rock without roots are those who expect homilies to stir their emotions, set the heart to flutter, bring tears to the eye, all with a message that escapes them. They come to hear oratorical fireworks. The seed among thorns are those who engage in a running debate with the homilist. They mentally contradict, correct and argue with the homily. Finally, there is the good soil that tries to hear the Word of God conveyed in a homily despite the static and accent of the homilist. A homily differs from a speech in that the Holy Spirit uses any homilist's words to speak a word of truth to us. We should not let the ideological or attitudinal accent of the homilist distract us from that word. We can learn to disregard the accent.

The people of faith, the good soil, are the ones from whom a harvest comes.

Point

God will insure that our fidelity and prayer are not wasted but will produce a harvest.

SATURDAY — Sixteenth Week of the Year
Jr 7:1-11   *Mt 13:24-30*

First Reading

The great reform undertaken by King Josiah was cut short by his tragic death. To the people it seemed to be a divine repudiation of his reformation. The king who followed Josiah began to return to the old ways. This is the setting for Jeremiah's famous Temple Sermon. He interprets this reversal of events. The people had started on the road to reformation and the restoration of the service of God when a series of political disasters hit them. Jeremiah cries out that reformation was more than liturgical. It was wrong to see the exactitude of ceremonial worship and reliance on a one-sided perception of the covenant as a divine warranty of protection. The flip side of reformation was the translation of the covenant into people's lives and their dealings with immigrants, orphans and widows. His unpopular assertion was that as long as this side of the covenant was not put into effect, the punishments of the Mosaic covenant would fall upon the people. He pictures the Temple as a den or hideout of thieves where people who defrauded others gather in the belief that they are safe from divine detection and judgment.

Gospel Reading

Jesus describes a moment of judgment in today's Gospel reading. Again, this is a message to the early Church as well as to us. There will always be mixed results in the Church's ministry. There will be false starts as well as great beginnings. The presence of the Holy Spirit with the Church is no insurance policy of absolute and total sanctity. The Lord reminds us indirectly not to become so preoccupied with the weeds that we forget about the good in the Church. We can become so obsessed by our sins that we fail to appreciate the enormous potential for good that we carry within ourselves. There will indeed come a time of judgment. Until then, we should continue to live out our faith as best we can.

Point

The Church lives by the faith of her people and not by her buildings.

MONDAY — Seventeenth Week of the Year
Jr 13:1-11   *Mt 13:31-35*

First Reading

One of the characteristics for which Jeremiah is renowned was his use of the dramatic gesture. He not only spoke words but enacted gestures that expressed his message with force and vigor. In this first reading, we have a strange gesture with a loincloth that rotted. The Lord tells Jeremiah and the people that the pride of Judah will "rot" as did the loincloth. On the one hand, Judah was as close to the Lord as such a garment is to a human being. Judah thought this covenant relationship guaranteed economic, political and institutional security. This was the source of her pride. That pride will be brought low. The covenant entailed responsibilities which Judah had disowned.

Gospel Reading

Jesus tells us that the reign of God is like yeast or a mustard seed that starts small and has a powerful effect. The reign of God exists with great vitality within the Church but is not restricted to the Church. We cannot take the Lord's words to us as a guarantee of continued growth in the number of believers. The reign of God can exist in many places outside the formal boundaries of the Church. Jesus tells us that where people try to follow God's word to them, His reign has a powerful effect.

Point

Covenant (old or new) is not a guarantee of wealth or political power. It is a promise that the good we do will always have power to save.

TUESDAY — Seventeenth Week of the Year
Jr 14:17-22   Mt 13:35-43

First Reading

Jeremiah views the devastation caused by the Babylonian armies throughout Judah and up to Jerusalem. His great role in the old covenant theology was to interpret the disasters that fell upon Judah—something the existing priests and prophets could not do. His message was that these events were not random and meaningless. Not only were they part of a larger design that made the world coherent, but these political traumas were God's judgment on Judah. It was a judgment for the national and individual sins of the people. It was a judgment for the interpretation of the covenant as a magical protective shield without corresponding duties by the people toward each other. It was a judgment for the popular rush toward melding pagan cults with authentic worship. Jeremiah's message was that this judgment was more than punishment. It had the larger purpose of healing. God alone had done all these things.

Gospel Reading

More than the other Gospels, Matthew focuses on the kingdom: where it is, what it looks like, who is in it, when it is coming, how it emerges. In today's Gospel reading, Jesus tells us that the work of building the kingdom is never over—the weeds are there to the very end. That is true as much on the individual level as on the larger stage of history. We might not face earthshaking conflicts but the struggle shows up every day in our dealings with others. When we experience these tensions of right and wrong, of God's presence and absence, we are experiencing the growing pains of Christ's kingdom inside us. The kingdom does not come in a blaze of glory; it is quietly at work like seed and yeast.

Point

Our frustrations, doubts, questions, sinning and repenting are all the growing pains of Christ coming to life in ourselves.

WEDNESDAY — Seventeenth Week of the Year
Jr 15:10, 16-21   *Mt 13:44-46*

First Reading

Jeremiah's career fell into two definable segments—neither of them very happy. The first was in the heyday of the great religious reformation of King Josiah. Jeremiah became disillusioned with the superficiality and subsequent gutting of the reform by Jehoiakim after Josiah's death. He withdrew from the public arena. Later, under the same reform-thwarting king, Jeremiah returned to tell of coming doom. He was rejected by his fellow-prophets, family and friends. He was evidently a gregarious person who was called to loneliness. He never married and fathered no children. His life was a living parable of Judah's spiritual isolation. No other prophet so touchingly and powerfully exposes the inside of his soul as does Jeremiah. Some have seen his suffering as a model of the passion of Jesus.

Today's first reading reveals the sense of frustration and loneliness that tore at his insides. He states that he has never borrowed nor lent to anyone (the best ways to make enemies) yet he is hated. The Lord reminds Jeremiah that his call is to oppose the sinfulness of the people and not to wallow in self-pity. Despite his popular rejection, Jeremiah is promised that he will survive and not be destroyed.

Gospel Reading

The emphasis of these two abbreviated images of the expensive pearl and the hidden treasure is on the discovery. In the last analysis, every person must find the Lord on his or her own. There is no special grove or shrine to which we have to journey. The longest journey is inward because God is within us as powerfully as He is in the rest of the universe. One vehicle for this inner entry is meditation. If we take the time to meditate, we will be undertaking the most ancient and demanding kind of pilgrimage where we are certain to find the Lord. Within ourselves, we discover His strength to live out the Gospel message.

Point

The longest, loneliest and most rewarding journey is the pilgrimage inward.

THURSDAY — Seventeenth Week of the Year
Jr 18:1-6   *Mt 13:47-53*

First Reading

God is a craftsman who shapes us much as the potter shapes clay. This was Jeremiah's reminder to the people of

Judah that they were not completely in charge of their own future. The political turnings of the time over which they had little control reminded them of this fact. Jeremiah asserts that in all of these political and military shifts, God is doing some shaping. Through the rhythm of defeat, exile and restoration, God is slowly fashioning a covenant community that will be spiritually grounded and not simply attached to the covenant's external formalities. We are all subject to circumstances beyond our control. Jeremiah's message to us as well is that God is using the events of our life to shape us into a holy people.

Gospel Reading

Jesus tells us that all kinds of fish are drawn from the sea into the net. All types of personalities join the Church for all sorts of reasons. Whatever an individual's motive, the vital issue is whether membership in the community Jesus founded changes that person in any fundamental way. God uses the events of our life to mold us. A living faith tries to see God's presence in each event. That very effort enables faith to mature. To be faithful does not mean that we remain glued to our faith as we experienced it on the day of our First Communion. In fact, when people abandon their faith, it is often because their life has changed while their understanding of the faith has not. It was a grammar school faith in an adult world. With such a lack of harmony, faith dropped to the side. The Christian community is the milieu in which our faith is nurtured and urged toward maturity through our social and spiritual interaction with others.

Point

If we look over the past twenty years of our life, we will catch a glimpse of the potter shaping the clay.

FRIDAY — Seventeenth Week of the Year
Jr 26:1-9
Mt 13:54-58

First Reading

This second half of the Book of Jeremiah is largely auto-biographical. The Temple Sermon ("a den of thieves") was recounted last week. This was Jeremiah's break with the twisted reversal of the Deuteronomic reform movement. To-day's reading is about prophets. Jeremiah speaks of coming destruction unless the people change in a serious way. His constant prediction of gloom has given birth to our modern word "jeremiad"—a recurrent message of disaster. But these were perilous times. Events were breaking quickly. The might of Babylon was on the horizon. Jeremiah tried in many ways to warn the people of inevitable destruction unless they turned from their suicidal public policies and life styles toward cove-nant living. It was an unpopular message that challenged cherished dogmas at a time when the court prophets were giving messages of cheer and quick recovery. When Jeremiah spoke of a coming destruction of Jerusalem similar to what had occurred to the northern shrine at Shiloh, they banned him from the Temple. Such a prophet was not welcome.

Gospel Reading

Jesus experiences the fate of the prophets in today's Gospel reading. The people of His hometown refused to pay much attention to His words. They knew His background too well. Too detached and extensive an analysis of the literary and religious story of the Gospel writings can cause the same reaction in ourselves. We come to fail to appreciate the glory, majesty and awesome power that Jesus promises us. When we take the Holy Spirit for granted, then the Gospel may well lose its power among us—until some event reshapes our understanding of it. If a prophet comes to tell the old story in a new way, we can be reborn.

Point

There are special times when our words—spoken in the right place, at the right time, to the right person, in the right way—become the word of the Lord to another human being. Then, in a small and special way, we become prophets.

SATURDAY — Seventeenth Week of the Year
Jr 26:11-16, 24   *Mt 14:1-12*

First Reading

We have a sort of mini-trial taking place in this first reading. Jeremiah had predicted devastation for an unrepentant Jerusalem while the professional prophets had proclaimed a coming prosperity. The professionals reject his defense that his message is from the Lord. The civil leaders and the people, on the other hand, sensed that his message deserved serious consideration. In their bones they knew that something in their society was seriously wrong. The outcome of this incident is ambiguous because Jeremiah was then kept in hiding so as not to be executed. Religious hatred is extremely potent. The shadow of the cross falls on the life of any person, even one sent by God, who challenges cherished orthodoxies.

Gospel Reading

The story of John the Baptist is a stark illustration of the conflict between God's word and human rebellion. John dared to challenge the vested interests and life style of the royal court. For John, the covenant and faith were not to be confined to

Temple services. They were to be applied indiscriminately. Like Jeremiah, John would not seek the easy way of the professional religious courtiers who told the government what it wanted to hear. For that refusal, he was executed in a particularly brutal way. This incident reminds us that Jesus' passion is drawing near. As Jeremiah and John upset religious complacency, so Jesus punctures spiritual and political somnolence to release a fresh awareness of our responsibilities as covenant people.

Point

Prophets reveal the cross and the cross reveals who are the true prophets.

MONDAY — Eighteenth Week of the Year
Jr 28:1-17   *Mt 14:13-21 (22-36)*

First Reading

In today's first reading, Hananiah, the professional prophet of good times predicts that Babylon's power will very soon be destroyed and happy days will return again in Judah. Jeremiah responds that such an outcome would be welcome news indeed but that the Lord's word to him was the very opposite of that. The sign of genuine prophecies in the past was not the foretelling of coming happiness but of the Lord's judgment. To show the inevitability of Babylon's domination, Jeremiah carried about a wooden yoke or harness as a dramatic symbol of God's judgment. Hananiah was so enraged by Jeremiah's challenge that he smashed the yoke. The Lord speaks through Jeremiah that for that single act of defiance, an iron yoke of greater servitude would be placed on Judah and that Hananiah in particular would perish.

Gospel Reading

In today's Gospel passage we have an equally dramatic symbol not of God's judgment but of His love. The supply of fish and loaves was meager, yet by the power of Christ all were satisfied. Today the Church offers bread and wine, resources that seem meager as well. Yet, by the power of the Holy Spirit, these bits of bread and drops of wine are transformed into Christ to give comfort, strength and light. Through this bread and wine, we share the same spirit as Christ.

(In a dramatic symbol of His care for people even in difficulty, Jesus comes to Peter over the water. As long as Peter kept faith in the Lord, he could walk on the water. When his attention turned from Jesus to the depths beneath him, he started to sink. This is a vivid illustration of the power of our baptismal link with Christ to enable us to endure severe difficulties.)

Jesus continues to give us strength and food.

Point

Through the food and strength the Lord gives us, we can feed and strengthen others.

TUESDAY — Eighteenth Week of the Year
Jr 30:1-2, 12-15, 18-22   Mt 14:22-36 (15:1-2, 10-14)

First Reading

"You shall be my people, I shall be your God." In this great prophetic oracle from the Book of Consolation (as chapters 30-33 are called), Jeremiah looks beyond the present tragedy that beset Judah to a time of healing and restoration. He speaks of a future princely leader who will risk his life to keep access to God open. Jeremiah sounds a major theme of his message— that history was not out of control. These tragedies were directed by the Lord for an ultimately saving purpose. The prediction of doom has become a prophetic constant not only in the classical prophets but in those of our own time as well. The world seems to be living on the edge of disaster and financial collapse. The message of Jeremiah to our own time is that beyond the sense of impending doom there is the possibility of revival. Beyond death, there is life. We shall not cease to be.

Gospel Reading

(Yesterday, Jesus was present in the storm.) Today, we have the Lord's pronouncement that cleanliness or corruption does not lie in the kinds of food we eat but in the kind of person we are within. There is a close connection between the miracle of the loaves, the calming of the storm, Peter's faith and his lack of it and our holiness within. To speak of inner peace is not vacuous and unverifiable. More destructive than the storms around us are those within us. The turbulence inside can cause everything we have built to fall apart. It was this absence of reconciliation within his nation's soul that troubled Jeremiah. The security Judah had sought was only external. The Lord has brought us the sacraments not only to bring order to the life of our world and Church but as instruments of unity within us as well.

Point

Jesus gives us that quiet center filled with Resurrection power from which we can see beyond the storm.

WEDNESDAY — Eighteenth Week of the Year
Jr 31:1-7   Mt 15:21-28

First Reading

Jeremiah announces a time when all the tribes of Israel and

Judah will again become a people under God. Jeremiah writes this from within the middle of a disaster. This was not fulfilled in a mechanically literal way. The Northern tribes never returned—they were absorbed into their neighbors. Still, this vision and assurance of God's age-old love is a powerful vision of His design for humanity as a whole. These words articulate a vision of that longed-for moment when all people will be united under the Fatherhood of God. They lift us beyond the power politics, spheres of interest and global conflicts of our time to a vision of God's will for our planet.

Gospel Reading

The pagan woman comes to Jesus for a healing miracle. He transcends the prejudices of His day and heals her child. The tiny dialogue we have can be variously interpreted because we have the words but not the music. We do not know whether the tone of His conversation is light banter, serious inquiry, rabbinic style or magisterial pronouncement. What is clear is that Jesus and the Canaanite woman both recognized a priority to be given to the Jews in His ministry. That was an historical fact. In this tiny vignette, Jesus races past Jeremiah's vision of Jewish unity toward a reuniting of mankind. Jesus is a universal Savior.

Point

Our differences should strengthen our unity and not generate division.

THURSDAY — Eighteenth Week of the Year
Jr 31:31-34   *Mt 16:13-23*

First Reading

Of the entire Book of Jeremiah, this passage is the most

well-known. It is probably the source of the title of the "New Testament (Covenant)." Jeremiah points to the heart of God's new arrangement with mankind. The covenant with Moses had been neglected during Israel's history as the covenant with David became trivialized into a popular source of bogus security for nation, cult and dynasty. The demands of the Mosaic covenant were met in mechanical ways, leading to a belief in automatic protection secured by external compliance. All of this was severely shaken when the North was exiled by Assyria. It will be given a second blow by Babylon's exile of the South. Here, Jeremiah gives a commanding vision. The covenant between God and people will be swept clean of its false foundations in Temple, dynasty, cult and law. It will be grounded in a new heart, fashioned by God's own spirit. It will effectively recreate humanity. This was the covenant that came to life in Jesus of Nazareth.

Gospel Reading

Peter's insight into Jesus as Messiah is followed by two events of great importance. Jesus places Peter and his faith at the foundation of the new covenant community that He had slowly been shaping during His ministry. Ecclesial faith is born! Jesus then shocks His disciples by announcing that the long awaited Messiah, the great Son of David, will have to suffer and die before His Resurrection to power. It was a vision of the future that had never entered their minds. Slowly they will see this come to be. That experience of the suffering, death and Resurrection of the Lord will forever temper the faith of the Church. The new covenant between God and people created by Jesus is a covenant that will always be deepened through time in a special way through suffering.

Point

The new link between God and people is not in a temple,

*king or state. Its ground is the suffering and Resurrection of
Jesus.*

FRIDAY — Eighteenth Week of the Year
Na 2:1, 3; 3:1-3, 6-7   *Mt 16:24-28*

First Reading

Nahum was a contemporary of Jeremiah. He announces
the final collapse of Nineveh, the capital of a greatly weakened
Assyria. Assyria, years before, had taken the Northern kingdom
of Israel into exile and gave great pain to the Southern kingdom
of Judah as well. Later, Babylon's growing power, with its own
fresh danger for Judah, would systematically destroy the Assyrian kingdom. Nahum describes very graphically the military
humbling of the once proud Assyrians. Nineveh had become a
symbol to Jews of oppression, hatred and evil (and is the
backdrop for the Jonah story). This oracle, called by some an
orgy of hatred, was to be a consolation for Judah as well as a
reminder that a kingdom built upon injustice, fraud and force,
as was Assyria, cannot last.

Gospel Reading

Jesus speaks about foundations that last: denying the desires of our superficial self for the salvation of our deeper core
within. The Lord tells us that to find our real self, we must
detach ourselves from the images and aspirations which our
culture imposes on us. This detachment requires that we fix our
sights on Christ to place everything in perspective. A life built
upon anything else (such as Assyria's greed and lust for power)
is a program for frustration. Nothing on earth can satisfy our
built-in yearning for God.

Point

Faith in Christ is not a beautiful aside. It is fundamental for healthful living.

SATURDAY — Eighteenth Week of the Year
Hab 1:12-2:4   *Mt 17:14-20*

First Reading

Habakkuk was another southern prophet who witnessed the shattering events of Jeremiah's time. He saw the extinction of one empire and the triumph of another. He pictures fishermen hauling in great numbers of fish. Because their tools were so effective they worship them. He uses this parable to condemn the kingdoms of Assyria and Babylon that worshipped power and war. For the first time in prophetic history, he asks whether history shows that "might is right" or that "right is might." These were questions the people of Judah were asking. They saw the reversal of their fortunes, the death of Josiah, ruthless pagans in triumph: the world they had been taught was divinely ordered seemed upside down. The answer would come in time with the fall of Babylon. Habakkuk stations himself as a watchman posing the question to God on the people's behalf. The Lord responds that the vision which carries the answer of the triumph of the righteous will come; it is not yet time. There will come a time when that word will come true. Now, the righteous will save themselves by living by faith rather than by sight.

Gospel Reading

Faith the size of a mustard seed can move mountains. The Lord's words are difficult for us to understand. Although we have faith and trust, so much of what we hope for fails to take place. How can we reconcile God's sovereignty, our aspirations of faith and the world as we know it? The faith which Jesus calls forth is a basic trust in God. It requires that we see the promises of God coming true in His own good time, of which we can only experience a down-payment in our lives.

Point

Faith is not wishful thinking. It is trust in the inevitable power of God.

MONDAY — Nineteenth Week of the Year
Ezk 1:2-5, 24-28   Mt 17:22-27

First Reading

Ezekiel is one of the strangest and most controversial figures of the Old Testament. He has been called the first fanatic in the Bible, one of the great spiritual figures of all time and the Father of Judaism. We find combined in him priest, prophet, poet, theologian, religious organizer and preacher. The Book of Ezekiel is filled with striking images, arresting symbolism and grotesque figures. Because it challenged the ideas of collective responsibility taught in the Torah, the old rabbis forbade anyone under thirty to read it. Today's first reading describes his call. Ezekiel was taken to Babylon with the first wave of deportees from Jerusalem, and it was in Babylon that he received his call to be a prophet. This odd reading immediately connects us to a major theme of his prophecy: the awesome majesty of God. Through symbols drawn from Israelite and Babylonian culture, Ezekiel experiences the living God. His message is that the great God of Israel and Judah has come to be with His people in exile. Thrones, fire, and electrum remind us of the mystery and magnificence of God.

Gospel Reading

In sharp contrast to today's first reading, the Gospel speaks about something that seems almost humiliating. Jesus pays the temple tax. Male Jews over 19 years of age were obligated to contribute to the Temple upkeep. We see the Son of Ezekiel's majestic God paying a Jewish version of pew rent. This brief scene reminds us that Jesus was like us in everything even in being taxed.

Easter and Pentecost mean that God came to our world to stay. The work of redemption and sanctification do not take place in some peaceful refuge in the heavens, but among us. This world is where the divine action is.

Point

Throughout the thousands of decisions we all make every year of our lives, God's design is coming to its fulfillment. That too is a sign of the power and majesty of God.

TUESDAY — Nineteenth Week of the Year
Ezk 2:8-3:4   *Mt 18:1-5, 10, 12-14*

First Reading

In this account of Ezekiel's call to be a prophet, his consumption of the scroll indicates that the divine message is now an intimate part of him. From this point, everything he says and does will be an integral expression of the message given to him. Every detail of his life will be an incarnation of God's word. In a non-theological sense, Ezekiel is now the word of God in the flesh. Repeatedly, he will be addressed by the Lord as "son of man." This phrase used throughout the Book of Ezekiel contrasts the lowliness of mankind with the august glory of God. Ezekiel is sent to address the house of Israel in exile. God's word is brought to people no matter where they are. There is no qualitative difference now between the exiles in Babylon and the remainder back in Judah. All are beloved of God and all are addressed by His word.

Gospel Reading

Jesus also speaks about His loving mission to all people. His words of life and grace are intended for every person, no matter where they are located financially, mentally or geographically. Jesus is in search of people wherever they are. That is also the mission of His disciples. We are to continue Jesus' search for His people to bring them His words of life and love. That simple searching is the profound fulfillment of our discipleship.

Point

Wherever people live, work and die should be the place where God's Word is present and powerfully preached.

WEDNESDAY — Nineteenth Week of the Year
Ezk 9:1-7; 10:18-22   *Mt 18:15-20*

First Reading

Although Ezekiel was living in Babylon, he was transported in the spirit to the Temple in Jerusalem which provides the setting for several of his visions. In one of these visions, he is alarmed by the abundance of pagan rituals taking place in the Temple as a matter of course. This is the background for today's first reading. A messenger is sent through Jerusalem to select those destined for punishment. Those marked with an "x" will be saved because they had decried the abominations practiced in the Temple. At the conclusion of this particular vision, Ezekiel witnessed the departure of the Lord's glory from the Temple. The glory that filled the Temple during Solomon's placement of the ark within it centuries before has departed and, very soon, the Temple will be destroyed. After a warning, the idolators are struck down as well. Repeatedly the prophets had condemned the worship of pagan gods with little effect. Warnings had been given but not heeded. This is a reminder to us that God never ambushes anyone. A prophetic warning is given to everyone.

Gospel Reading

Today's Gospel reading is about fraternal correction. Jesus describes a rudimentary form of due process. If someone appears to be doing wrong, speak to him or her. If that fails, bring a witness. If that does not work, refer the matter to the local Church. The Lord is showing us that there is a Christian way of settling problems. If discussion does not help, there are alternatives. Private resolution should always be the first step before we initiate a public process or litigation. Fraternal correction is never easy to give or to receive. Some spiritual directors suggest that each of us have a "truth speaker" in our lives—an individual we trust who can speak directly, freely and candidly to us about any personal shortcoming in our life.

Whenever Christians gather to pray, discuss, disagree or to correct one another, the Lord Jesus is still among us.

Point

No area of our life, not even our disagreements, should be cut off from the healing presence of Christ.

THURSDAY — Nineteenth Week of the Year
Ezk 12:1-2   *Mt 18:21-19:1*

First Reading

Today's first reading provides deep background information for the Gospel section. In this short selection, we are reminded that Ezekiel's preaching was not easy. He is called to speak less to an apathetic house (which has its own share of difficulties) than to a rebellious house. What he has to say will go against the grain. There was an enormous gap between the message which Ezekiel was sent to deliver and the psychological and religious condition of the people.

Gospel Reading

Jesus' parables also speak to the gap between God's word and our faith. Throughout Matthew's Gospel, Jesus describes the life of the kingdom, the Spirit-filled life. The demanding ideals which He articulates with such vigor serve as measuring rods by which we can tell how far we are from the kingdom of God as a dimension of our life. In yesterday's reading, Jesus told us that we should be ready to heal our quarrels. In today's reading, Peter asks how frequently we should do so. "How many times?" Jesus responds, in effect, "All the time!" That is a very hard saying for us. To underscore His point, Jesus recounts a parable which contrasts the huge debt forgiven by a king with the repayment of nickels and dimes which the forgiven official refused to postpone. The point made is that we find it difficult to forgive big things or small yet we expect forgiveness from God all the time. The assurance of sacramental confession is that He will forgive us. We expect it. We plan on it. Jesus tells us that if an individual admits himself or herself to be a sinner and has experienced forgiveness and reconciliation with the Father, they should not be unbending toward others.

Point

Our willingness to forgive others is one empirical test of our personal distance from the kingdom of God in our lives.

FRIDAY — Nineteenth Week of the Year
Ezk 16:1-15, 60, 63, (59-63)   *Mt 19:3-12*

First Reading

In today's first reading, Ezekiel tells the story of Jerusalem and its rise from a tiny, corrupt backwater pagan town to the corrupt grand capital of David's kingdom. He frames it as an allegory like a motion picture from the 40's. A wealthy man finds a young girl in the gutter. He cleans her up, gives her everything and then she leaves him for someone else. In the section between verses 15 and 60, omitted from the reading, Ezekiel describes her activities in graphic terms that prudes might call "pornographic." It does catch one's attention.

Ezekiel sees the relationship between God and Jerusalem as a marriage that had broken down. God remains faithful and ready to heal His wanton people. Ezekiel's core message is that God will not abandon His people despite their sin.

Gospel Reading

There was a discussion among rabbis concerning the grounds for divorce. The liberal school of Hillel allowed divorce for any reason, even the most trivial. The strict school of Shammai allowed a bill of divorce only for adultery. Jesus is pulled into the debate and refers back to Genesis as evidence of God's will for marriage. The divorce allowed by Moses as an exception had by now become the rule. The Lord presents the kingdom vision for married life. That ideal should be a fact in our world. For several reasons it is not. Today, as Ezekiel's allegory comes to life, marriages break down. It is a serious question as to how the community Jesus founded should respond to this regrettable phenomenon, especially in the light of His mandate that we forgive seventy times seven.

The breakdown of any marriage is a tragedy. Yet, severed spouses remain Catholics, members of Christ's body. They are the wounded members most in need of aid and healing from others. We should help them to keep faith and hope alive.

Point

However much we fail the Lord, His people should be willing to welcome us back home.

SATURDAY — Nineteenth Week of the Year
Ezk 18:1-10, 13, 30-32   *Mt 19:13-15*

First Reading

There are many ways of evading our responsibility before God. Frequently we shift the reason for our failures to our environment, family or life's proverbial unfairness. This was part of the meaning of the proverb quoted in today's first reading. The father eats sour grapes, the children get the sour stomach. Ezekiel attacks an attitude prevalent among the exiles—that they were bearing the consequences of their ancestors' sins. Earlier generations, they felt, were responsible for the debacle of Judah's exile. Ezekiel reminds them that every generation has its own accounting before God. If we accept the benefits of past injustice, we become liable for the judgment upon that injustice. This is a new note of individual responsibility before God. We are part of a larger community of faith and of sin. Before God we are each responsible for our own deeds and misdeeds. We also share in the larger context of society's wrongdoing either through our silence or acquiescence. Ezekiel underscores the responsibility of the present generation before God. We cannot shift liability to the past. We must account to God for what we are and what we will become.

Gospel Reading

The focus of this little incident is less on Jesus' approachability than on the qualifications for entry into the kingdom. Just as children in those days (we suppose) accepted the low place they were given in society, so the condition for entry into the kingdom is a recognition of our real standing before God. This requires that we appreciate not only the good we have done but also the sin in our life. To enter God's kingdom requires that we realize with ruthless honesty our moral condition. We are disciples not simply because of our parents and friends but by our own choice. Honesty in self-analysis is a requirement for serious spiritual growth.

Point

We enter or leave the Lord's presence on our own two feet. Nobody can do it for us.

MONDAY — Twentieth Week of the Year
Ezk 24:15-24
Mt 19:16-22

First Reading

This remarkable passage from Ezekiel shows his profound faith in his prophetic call. Everything in his life became a way of urging his message onto the people in exile. His wife, the "delight of his eyes," had died suddenly. Ezekiel used this personal tragedy and his public grief as a way of continuing to call the people to repent and avoid national grief for their sins. He alludes to the coming destruction of the Jerusalem Temple. That Temple had become the symbol of everything the Jewish people saw as unique to themselves: covenant, law, worship, election. Yet that Temple was profaned by the quasi-pagan practices that took place within. One of Ezekiel's visions had already been of the departure of the Lord's glory from the Temple. Now, he predicts that this revered building and national center would be taken from the people's eyes. The "delight of their eyes" would be gone and they would mourn. The Temple had been built as a physical reminder of the covenant. After that covenant had been broken by the people, the Temple ceased to have a purpose. Spiritually, it had become an empty shell.

Gospel Reading

The young man wanted more out of religion than the prescriptions and prohibitions of the Commandments. Like many people today, he wanted to experience the inner light of the Spirit and to closely integrate faith and life in his personality so as not to be jerked back and forth by events. Jesus instructs him to surrender everything he has and to follow Him. The issue here is not wealth but discipleship. Giving up property does not automatically make us followers of Christ. It is the life of discipleship in deed, word and thought that leads to eternal life. That kind of discipleship entails the profoundly personal decision to actively follow the Lord as well as the difficult work of weaving that decision into a concrete program of life.

Point

Follow-through is a very difficult step. It was the point at which the people of Judah wandered away and the young man departed.

TUESDAY — Twentieth Week of the Year
Ezk 28:1-10   *Mt 19:23-30*

First Reading

This passage is heavy with irony as Ezekiel describes the coming destruction of the King of Tyre. He had been a major commercial and minor military success. He joined an anti-Babylonian alliance and was now about to face an enraged Babylon. Within this little melodrama of failed political strategies, Ezekiel sees a deeper cause for this king's coming destruction. His reliance on the wealth and assets he had accumulated, together with the assumption that his success was due to his own charm and savvy, were the Achilles' heel of his life. Frequently, a sudden disaster reminds us of the fact that we are creatures—fragile, limited, human beings who, despite our marvelous superiority over the rest of creation, remain in the power of events and forces beyond our control. The King of Tyre's vice was not his material success. It was his deification of that success as a comprehensive definition of everything he was.

Gospel Reading

The disciples were overwhelmed by Jesus' statement that a camel can sail through a needle's eye with greater ease than the wealthy can enter heaven. Their reaction was based on the Old Testament assumption that wealth and prosperity were indicators of God's favor. If prosperous people, so evidently blessed by God, cannot be saved, then the poor of the land are almost certainly damned. Jesus assures them that with God's help anyone can be saved. Following the Lord is a serious affair that involves a great deal more than keeping the Commandments. A person can become so wrapped in career, financial success, his or her own intellectual virtuosity or charm that these things occupy the center of life rather than one's relationship to the Lord.

The experience of God's kingdom is available to anyone willing to break out and into it. The barriers are in our own minds and hearts.

Point

The experience of Christ's kingship over our lives and the freedom it brings are available to every person.

WEDNESDAY — Twentieth Week of the Year
Ezk 34:1-11   *Mt 20:1-16*

First Reading

Ezekiel delivers a stinging rebuke to the shepherds of Judah. The political leaders who had been divinely commissioned to lead the people into a deeper knowledge of the God of Sinai and Abraham had used their position to line their own pockets. Because their lives were poured into self-service rather than true service, they fall under Ezekiel's most terrible condemnation. The Lord announces through him that they will be removed. Now God will shepherd His people. The phrase is reminiscent of the New Testament theme of the Good Shepherd. Significantly, it is a rejection of the king as the one through whom God's blessing would flow to the people. Ezekiel looks to a time when intermediaries will disappear and God will guide each heart and life into a deeper knowledge of Himself. In that new age, priests will be instruments of the Spirit, who will be directly available to all people. A hierarchy will no longer serve as filters through whom God's Spirit passes to others.

Gospel Reading

We can read this parable on two levels: why Matthew put it in his Gospel; and what its significance is for us. Matthew probably includes this parable because of a local conflict between the Jewish Christians who had entered the Church first and the burgeoning number of later Gentile entrants. Jesus' words that the last to come are as important as the first to arrive are a lesson to Church stalwarts that all people are invited to drink deeply from the living water. We read this parable to learn that closeness to the kingdom, our personal holiness, is not determined by how long we have been Catholic or, as Ezekiel reminds us, by our rank in the community. Closeness to the kingdom is determined by how responsive we are to the Lord's call. The point of the parable is not how long the laborers worked but that they answered the call.

Point

It is not status, age or function but closeness to the Lord that gives a person spiritual power.

THURSDAY — Twentieth Week of the Year
Ezk 36:23-28   *Mt 22:1-14*

First Reading

The language of restoration and of covenant emphasized to the people of Judah their very special spiritual position. This is also language that people today love to twist into a justification of Middle East politics. The language of promise sank into Jewish minds, hearts and culture. They knew themselves as God's chosen people, a nation with a promise. This was a title they loved. With that title, however, came the responsibilities of fidelity, bearing witness and obedience to God's word. This is the point at which the covenant broke down. It brings us to the heart of the Gospel parable.

Gospel Reading

We can ask our two questions (why Matthew recalled it and its meaning for us) of this parable. The people of the covenant had refused the invitation to its deeper fulfillment that was offered in Jesus. They refused to take the next step beyond law and national boundaries toward which Jesus called them. He then opened the kingdom to the outcasts—those who knew their need for God. The meaning of the parable for us is that the Gospel is preached today through all sorts of media. People hear the words and refuse the invitation for all sorts of reasons. Still, acceptance is not enough. The wedding garment indicates that acceptance entails discipleship. The test of the sincerity of our acceptance of God's love is the extent to which it changes us. The "born again" experience (or any profoundly emotional religious experience) is authenticated by the extent to which it expresses itself in our lives. Otherwise, such an experience is simply an emotional release but not the start of a new way of life. The darkness in the parable can mean the point when we have to live with the spiritual consequences of our refusal to be disciples.

Point

The call of Christ is a challenge not a game.

FRIDAY — Twentieth Week of the Year
Ezk 37:1-14   *Mt 22:34-40*

First Reading

This is the most vivid and famous of Ezekiel's visions: the

valley of the "born again" bones. It is a powerful vision of the ability of God's Spirit to restore life. The broken bones signify Israel and Judah. The people were broken, dead in spirit and scattered all over the known world in the diaspora. Suddenly, the bones start to gather. One bone connects to another. Sinews appear. Finally, the Spirit of God rushes through to give them new life and a people are restored. Ezekiel used this vision to show a despondent people that God would raise them up and inject new life into them. That vision of Ezekiel came true in the Church.

Gospel Reading

The theme of the Gospel readings this week has been the reality of the spiritual domain. It is as much a real part of an individual's make-up as is one's intellect or social network. Yet, it is neglected. A person can be a theological giant while remaining a spiritual midget. Some people let this part of themselves atrophy until all that is left is dry bone. The spiritual life is dynamic, however, and its development requires method, discipline and practice. It has plateaus of achievement and predictable sequences of crises. The question of the young man haunts us. What must I do? There is a great deal more to the spiritual life than keeping the Commandments. There is the experience of the kingdom, access to which comes not with decision but discipleship—that slow and gradual process by which we translate the two great Commandments into our lives in thousands of ways. On these two great pillars of love of God and of neighbor everything rests: Law, prophets and the spiritual life.

Point

So often we go through the motions of faith. The Spirit of God can bring those gestures to life.

SATURDAY — Twentieth Week of the Year
Ezk 43:1-7   *Mt 23:1-12*

First Reading

Ezekiel's message to the exiled Jews was that their restoration as a covenant community will not come from brand new political leadership. It will come from the infusion of God's Spirit among the people. In these last chapters of the Book of Ezekiel, we have a detailed outline of this restored community. He sees a time of reinvigorated Judaism when justice and faith will pervade the people. It will be a new event wrought by God and not by any political leader. Judaism had seen by now the frailty of its leaders. In this vision, Ezekiel sees a restored Temple. The glory of the Lord that he had seen depart years before now returns to again reside in the Temple. There is a difference. The Lord's glory will now dwell not only in the Temple but in the hearts of individuals to provide a close link between religion and life. This vision looks past the survival of post-exilic Judaism into the new kingdom of Jesus where He is at once Temple, priest and sacrifice.

Gospel Reading

Jesus speaks reverently of the teaching institution in Israel. That office by which the Torah Law was transmitted to the people was vital for the survival of the holy traditions. The Lord distinguishes between the institution and its occupants. He cautions His disciples against following the life style of the Pharisees. His warning coincides with the vision of Ezekiel. No longer would the holiness of the new covenant community depend on the holiness of priest or teacher. The communication of the Spirit is direct. The leader and teacher is the Lord. Everyone else who occupies a position in the Church is in some way a vicar of Jesus. He is Jesus' agent, not His substitute. There is no replacement for faith in the Lord Jesus as the way to salvation. The mark of true honor in the Church, correlatively, is service to others.

Point

The Church coheres through the Holy Spirit of Christ and not through human charisma.

MONDAY — Twenty-First Week of the Year
2 Th 1:1-5, 11-12   *Mt 23:13-22*

First Reading

The Thessalonian letters are the oldest of the New Testament writings. They were composed about twenty-five years after the Lord's Resurrection and reveal the extraordinary preoccupation of these churches with the Second Coming of Jesus. Paul's first letter had caused a great deal of anxiety and social disarray with its discussion of the imminent return of the Lord. This second letter was written to calm and clarify the situation. In this reading, Paul begins by giving thanks to God for the Thessalonian Christians. He does not praise their apocalyptic hysteria but their continuing faith and mutual love. He points to the quality of their daily community life as an example to be held up to the other churches. So frequently, we consider the impact of our faith on the world at large. It is important as well to consider the effect a parish has on the other parishes around it. The vitality and dynamism of a particular Christian community can have a great and energizing impact on its neighbors. To the extent that we share our faith experiences and community story with others, we can provide models upon which other parishes can draw as they build up their faith.

Gospel Reading

Each of the Gospels emerged from individual faith communities which preserved various emphases of Jesus' teaching.
This section was preserved by Jewish Christians in Palestine-
Syria because of the tensions that flared up between them and
the synagogue Pharisees. The Lord describes the top-heavy
religion that concerned itself with minute details while forgetting the basic reason for its existence. The result was a theology
without faith. Jesus tells us to restore balance by looking to our
one teacher—Himself. If we keep the Lord at the center of our
spiritual and ecclesial life, we will not be easily distracted by
speculation about the end of the world nor by the intricacies of
church customs. There is one Teacher at the center.

Point

*In Jesus Christ alone does our religious behavior find its
heart and soul.*

TUESDAY — Twenty-First Week of the Year
2 Th 2:1-3, 14-16   *Mt 23:23-26*

First Reading

The Thessalonian preoccupation with the end of the world
is a mood with which we can easily identify. There is a great
deal of speculation in our time about the emerging signs of the
final scenario. Religious bookstores are filled with publications
on the topic. The second-coming scare among these early
Christians was triggered by some kind of oracular utterance,
rumor or fake letter alleged to be from Paul. It has been remarked that perhaps Paul's earlier discussion about the *sudden*

return of the Lord was misinterpreted to mean an *immediate* return. The resultant anxiety had disconcerting spiritual and social effects among the members of the community. It is this anxiety that Paul addresses. In a section omitted from today's reading, he describes an extended set of events that will occur before the return of the Lord in order to calm fears of a quick end as well as to show that a great deal of Christian missionary work has yet to come. The Church cannot simply fold its hands and wait for the cosmic finale. Paul advises the Christians to hold to the traditions they have received from him. As theological and cultural patterns change, it is important that we have a firm grasp on the meaning of our tradition as a secure base upon which to anchor our individual and parish lives. Without such an anchor in the tradition (as opposed to the conventions of the Church), we can be victimized by passing theological excitements.

Gospel Reading

If it is clear that we cannot short-circuit our duty to seek justice in the world by waiting for the Lord's return, it is equally clear that we cannot truncate our struggle for holiness by observance of ritual gesture alone. The holiness to which Jesus invites us requires the conforming of our minds and hearts to God. The Pharisaic vice is a preoccupation with the minutiae of external observance in the belief that what we can see is more important or equivalent to the part of us which we cannot see. The Lord reminds us that there is no shortcut to sanctity.

Point

There is no easy back door into the kingdom experience of Christ.

WEDNESDAY — Twenty-First Week of the Year
2 Th 3:6-10, 16-18   *Mt 23:27-32*

First Reading

Preoccupation with the coming end of the world led to a general ennervation among some Christians as their interest in secular affairs fell to a zero point. The effort to achieve justice, to spread the Gospel, to seek interior renewal, to pattern their daily lives on the Lord Jesus were all placed on "hold" as they awaited His return to set everything right. This is a negative side-effect of excessive speculation about the "last things." One can become so preoccupied with the world to come as to diminish any interest in the world in which we live. Zealots obsessed with the coming end of the world show little interest in human rights, corporate behavior, or morality in foreign or domestic policy. Paul never saw faith and hope in the Lord's coming as a rationale for neglecting our obligations in this world. In fact, Jesus' return as Judge requires a vibrant missionary zeal to transform and change our world in preparation for His coming. Paul's prescription that those who do not work should not eat was not the indictment of governmental social programs it is regrettably interpreted to be. It was, rather, intended as a corrective to that social lassitude deriving from excessively apocalyptic thinking.

Gospel Reading

Jesus excoriates the hypocrisy of the Pharisees and scribes as they romanticize and lament the faith of days gone by. He insists that faith in the present is the determining factor of our salvation. To lament a lost golden age or to project a golden future can shift attention from the holiness or sin of the "now." The Pharisees hymned ancient heroes and spoke of what might have been. It is a great temptation to retroject ourselves into an abstract past or to project ourselves into an unfinished future as a way of avoiding the challenging complexity of the present. The judgment of the Lord is in the now.

Point

Past and future revolve around the present. The past has brought us to the present which is the point from which we approach the future.

THURSDAY — Twenty-First Week of the Year
1 Cor 1:1-9   *Mt 24:42-51*

First Reading

We begin Paul's first letter to the Corinthians, one of the most famous and frequently quoted of his epistles. It is among the most revealing of his writings in which he gives expression to a full gamut of emotions. Theological argument, exhortation, rebuke, practical advice and soaring poetry all interweave as he darts among issues in his effort to shepherd this feisty Corinthian community closer to the Lord. The letter also tells us a great deal about one of the most vigorous of early Christian churches. In this letter, we have a peek into the politics, loves, hates and strains of an early Christian community. In today's reading, Paul begins by praising the rich and diverse endowments of the Corinthian Christians. Their many gifts, diverse charisms and enormous spiritual energy show how the Spirit was working among them in many ways. The task facing Paul was to try to unify this heterogeneity into a single community under the Lordship of Jesus. It is a task for any parish.

Gospel Reading

The real function of the second coming is found in Jesus' words in today's Gospel reading. It gives us perspective. Realization that the Master will return for a strict accounting enables us, both as a parish and as individuals, to separate the trivial from the important. The Lord's second coming reminds us that the Church is an interim instrument. Everything of her—dioceses, parishes, liturgy committees, personnel boards, finance committees, diocesan offices—are all intended to glorify the Lord Jesus. In the final analysis, our manner of dealing with one another is the ultimate sign of faith that we can offer the world. If the law of the jungle pervades a diocese, then why should the world listen?

Point

The test which places things in perspective is whether our parish membership helps us to love God and our neighbor—or not.

FRIDAY — Twenty-First Week of the Year
1 Cor 1:17-25   *Mt 25:1-13*

First Reading

The Corinthian Church was a real potpourri. It was composed of an educated elite as well as a broad cross-section of typical Corinthian society. A string of Christian evangelists came through periodically on different preaching circuits. Paul makes it clear in today's first reading that he was not sent to baptize or shepherd a local community as a pastor. His function was one of evangelizing. He preached, aroused interest in the Gospel, motivated the people, planted a seed organization and then left it to others to establish the community on an ongoing basis. Quite a few preachers were wending their way through Corinth. Paul reminds the people that the important value is that the Gospel be preached and not the particular preacher. Buzz words ("wisdom"), razzle-dazzle and gimmicks can interfere with a serious commitment to the Lord. Once a fiery, attractive or suave evangelizer has departed, the decision that confronts each person remains the cross of Christ. The real act of faith is not in an individual preacher but between the crucified Lord and ourselves. The depth of that faith in Christ affects the rest of our lives.

Gospel Reading

Jesus' parable complements Paul's message about decision. Our present actions have consequences for the future. Even inaction has consequences. The wisdom or foolishness with which we conduct our lives have implications which we cannot escape. The passion or heat of the moment can distort things now as well as in the future. No argument is ever really forgotten. The good we do, individually and collectively, and the good we fail to do, are part of us. Nothing is ever a complete throwaway. Every day, we are either building up the kingdom or destroying it.

Point

Our present decisions and indecisions are never trivial.

SATURDAY — Twenty-First Week of the Year
1 Cor 1:26-31
Mt 25:14-30

First Reading

Paul gives a personal profile of the Corinthian Christians. He emphasizes the fact that few, if any, were high-rollers, movers or shakers. They were ordinary folks. Yet God entrusted to them the great message of planetary salvation and His very power to effect that salvation. The sanctifying power of the God of the universe was given to them not only to show the rest of the world that such power and peace are gifts, but also to make it clear to these Corinthians that whatever spiritual superiority they enjoy is from the Lord. If there is boasting to do, let them boast in the Lord Jesus. The result of all this is that there is little place among them for divisions. Since their glory and spiritual gifts are from the Lord, they should recognize their common giftedness and find in that a basis for unity and common praise rather than division.

Gospel Reading

The Spirit we have received can expand the talents we have been given. Each of us has unique abilities and perspectives that we bring to bear upon our parish communities. Those talents can be developed as they are used and can be enriched by our interaction with others. Further, the Holy Spirit enables us to turn our gifts into apostolic instruments for the edification of others and the glorification of the Lord Jesus. All that we are and have can be influenced by the Spirit. To cut off any part of ourselves from His presence is to hide a talent that might build up the body of Christ. For such reticence we are accountable to the Lord.

Point

Everything we have, including our past mistakes, can be turned by the Holy Spirit into an instrument of grace.

MONDAY — Twenty-Second Week of the Year
1 Cor 2:1-5   *Lk 4:16-30*

First Reading

Today's readings are about preaching. Paul insists that any effect of his preaching flowed not from persuasive and adroit argument but from the convincing power of the Holy Spirit. Every preacher experiences the phenomenon of a technically perfect homily, delivered with gusto, which still falls flat with little or no impact. At other times, words simply spoken from the heart seem to touch people in a deeply personal way. For some reason they work and the Spirit moves.

The homilies we can recall, perhaps only in bits and pieces, were probably not delivered by exceptional or celebrated speakers. Yet something of their words have remained with us and perhaps have changed us as well. The Spirit works through the speaker. Simple words can strike us with enormous force if we are willing to listen.

Gospel Reading

In the oldest account we have of a synagogue service, the Lord Jesus delivers His first homily at Nazareth and the people, initially enthusiastic, are then unwilling to listen. As Jesus quoted Isaiah's message to the poor and outcast, a theme of Luke's Gospel, the audience focused on His background rather than His words. They were not receptive to His message. Jesus reminds them that in the Old Testament, two pagans received the mercy and healing of God through the prophets Elijah and Elisha because they were open to that Word. Such an accusation caused the people to become violent and to eject Him, thereby proving His charge against them. This scene captures in small swift strokes the story of Jesus' ministry in Galilee and Judea.

Frequently, we reject a preacher because he does not use the correct buzz words or is on the wrong side of an imaginary line. Still, the Holy Spirit speaks through every homily. The homily is not an interruption of the Mass which we can easily skip. It is an integral part of the liturgy through which the Spirit can touch us.

Point

The Holy Spirit speaks through any word to those willing to listen.

TUESDAY — Twenty-Second Week of the Year
1 Cor 2:10-16   Lk 4:31-37

First Reading

One word that has been used to describe Christian living is "journey." An older and perhaps more applicable word is "struggle." Paul describes the struggle between the Spirit of Christ and the spirit of the world. It is an experience we all might have felt as we are torn by the dilemmas of our life. Such a struggle can eventuate in growth toward Christian maturity and wisdom. It enables us to rise above the spirituality and outlook we had in grammar school as we develop the spiritual tools, criteria, mechanisms and strategies for dealing with adult life in a Christian way. These are the materials of an appraisal of spiritual and secular things that Paul describes. Their use results in our gradual approximation to the mind of Christ. Slowly, we begin to be able to think like the Lord.

Gospel Reading

The closer we are to the mind of Christ, the more dramatic is the struggle we have with the spirit of the world. This is one reason why the Lord's confrontations with Satan and the evil spirits in the Gospels are so stark and brutal. We are witnessing in them the collision of two opposites. This is why the saints were very conscious of sin and more aware of wrongdoing in the slightest things than are most people. The light of Christ floods our minds revealing little scrapes and scars that otherwise we would never have noticed. This inner light constitutes the difference between Francis of Assisi and Jack the

Ripper. The struggle to put on the mind of Christ is a fact of Christian life. The mind of Christ is a good deal more than "best intentions"; it is the same wisdom, intelligence and know-how that we see the Lord exercising throughout the Gospels.

Point

Putting on the mind of Christ emerges out of the struggle between the Spirit of Christ and the spirit of the world.

WEDNESDAY — Twenty-Second Week of the Year
1 Cor 3:1-9   *Lk 4:38-44*

First Reading

Today's reading sharpens up one of the problems that existed in the Corinthian community. It was a tension between the followers of Paul and of Apollos. It seems that Paul had laid the groundwork of Gospel living as an evangelizer. Apollos followed to elaborate this basic teaching. It seems that he opened new horizons and presented an exciting and perhaps off-beat message. The people were deeply impressed by Apollos. Paul insists that he laid foundations upon which Apollos built. He planted what another watered. Paul uses this to upbraid the spiritual immaturity of the Corinthians as evidenced by the factions that divided them. The religious "groupies" among them were more dazzled by the procession of messengers than by the core message. In such personality cults, they missed the central figure of all evangelism: the Lord Jesus. If we place our common Lord at our center, we will be able to reconcile our differences.

Gospel Reading

Jesus also refused to allow His miracles (which He used to

concretize His message) to distract from His fundamental message. He realized that a variety of Messianic expectations swirled about in Galilee. There were many people ready to pour His message into prefabricated molds that conformed to what they expected a proper Messiah to be. For this reason, the Lord is unusually careful about the way He is named, addressed and described. It was crucial that nothing detract from the fundamentally spiritual, and therefore revolutionary, message He brought concerning the reign of God. The personal impact on individuals was most important. Personal depth of faith came first, although it would be authenticated by the way it was lived out in society. Jesus sternly refused to reverse that priority.

Point

Everything flows from our relationship with the Lord.

THURSDAY — Twenty-Second Week of the Year
1 Cor 3:18-23   *Lk 5:1-11*

First Reading

After Apollos' spectacular preaching, the Corinthian Christians saw themselves as spiritually sophisticated. Paul disabuses them of that claim. Their internal divisions showed a great deal of spiritual immaturity. Note the inversion in today's reading. At the start, the Corinthians boasted that one belonged to Paul or Apollos. Here, Paul asserts that the Christians do not belong to the minister. The minister is sent to serve them. Priests and bishops belong to the people and the people belong to Christ who belongs to the Father. Paul states, in effect, that the Church is ultimately God's operation. One disciple plants, another waters but God gives the growth. All the public relations programs that can be devised cannot produce a single sincere act of faith, one genuine act of repentance, a single authentic conversion. We prepare the way and God does the rest.

Gospel Reading

In today's Gospel reading, Jesus gives a catch of fish to the first disciples and makes them fishers of mankind. Their story will be told in the Acts of the Apostles. It is a great error to believe that we produce salvation. It is a contemporary form of neo-Pelagianism to claim that enough money, programs, meetings, and policy statements will save people. The opposite error is to claim that we can simply sit by and allow the Holy Spirit to build up the Church, as though our industry and intelligence were irrelevant. This is a form of neo-Quietism. There is no excuse for a sloppy ministry. We provide the nets and skills. The Lord provides the catch.

Point

As a parish and as individuals, we plant and nourish while God gives the growth.

FRIDAY — Twenty-Second Week of the Year
1 Cor 4:1-5   *Lk 5:33-39*

First Reading

Paul concludes a long section of the letter in which he justifies his work among the Corinthians. He is emphatic that apostles are simply managers and agents of the mysteries of God. Their responsibility is to be faithful to Jesus' message and to follow His call. Only the Lord can accurately judge how faithful we have been. The same is true of every Christian. The

Lord called us at our baptism and continues to invite us to deeper commitment at different stages of our life. If a person has been an active Catholic, a circumstance may arise through which Christ calls him or her to a more prayerful, contemplative spirituality for a while. In the case of an intensely devotional Catholic, events may arise through which the Lord calls him or her to a more active and aggressive apostolate. Our obligation is to do what Christ wants. He alone can judge how faithful we have been.

Gospel Reading

Jesus' continual call to us is also a point that can be drawn from today's Gospel reading of new wine in fresh skins. If we remain too rigidly tied to our past, we will be unable to hold, sustain or release the vitality of the new grace, power and direction toward which Jesus is calling us. Just as the Gospel was not reducible to synagogue or Jerusalem Judaism, so circumstances change, we change and the contexts in which the Gospel must be lived and preached change. In the middle of all this, the Lord is not silent. We should remain attuned, through prayer and spiritual conversation with others, to the Lord's call to us.

Point

We are called to be faithful to the Lord. Despite what others may think, He alone knows the real depth of our fidelity to Him.

SATURDAY — Twenty-Second Week of the Year
1 Cor 4:9-15   *Lk 6:1-5*

First Reading

Paul concludes his self-defense with a stab at constructive

irony and an affirmation of the special place he holds in the Corinthians' spiritual story. To counterpoint their self-inflation, Paul contrasts the vilification, poverty and difficult life he lives as an apostle with the exalted boasts the Corinthians make for themselves. Paul is called to the great mission of giving birth to Christians. They are called to the work of rearing his spiritual children. Ironically, they have lost the sense of their own spiritual need and reliance upon the grace of Christ. They are simply tools of the power of God. He concludes by claiming a special place among them because it was through him that they received the Gospel. He was the founding father of the Corinthian church who set the basic tone of their spirituality. They were to be a Pauline Christian community—that is, bound not by law but by grace and faith.

Gospel Reading

Many of the events in the Gospels are reported to make a point not only to the various early Christian communities but to make a point valid for all time. Jesus is the founder of the Christian community. His attitudes toward Law, Sabbath and religious observances are normative for all Christians at all times. For this reason, the story of grain-picking on the Sabbath was retold to show that Jesus' attitude toward Sabbath Law did not share the absolutist, obsessive quality that Pharisaic legalism had imposed on it. The Lord saw the Sabbath as celebrative of our liberation from sin and our new relationship with the Father. He refused to turn it into a burden that would cage people into a new slavery. This attitude remains normative for us.

Point

The attitudes of the Lord Jesus set the tone for all of Christian spirituality on all points of the ecclesiastical spectrum.

MONDAY — Twenty-Third Week of the Year
1 Cor 5:1-8   *Lk 6:6-11*

First Reading

Paul devotes this section of the Corinthian letter to several specific issues that had torn the community apart. The first case is that of "lewd conduct"—possibly a man living with his stepmother. It may have been that some Corinthians were not disturbed by such behavior but viewed it as an instance of following one's conscience in the Lord without any external guidelines arbitrarily imposed to cabin one's new freedom in Christ. Paul is shocked by such a laissez-faire morality and, in effect, excommunicates the individual. He excludes him from the Christian community in the hope that this might bring the man to his senses. Paul is causing temporary discomfort for the sake of a permanent improvement. It is in this light that Church penalties should be seen and administered. They are not punishments but rehabilitative instruments to bring an individual to appreciate the corrosive effect his conduct has on the community life of a parish. Tolerance of such highly individual and seemingly isolated instances, Paul asserts, can lead to a gradual sclerosis of a community's moral sensibilities. A little yeast can leaven all the dough.

Gospel Reading

Jesus probes more deeply into the meaning of Sabbath observance and of religion generally. His statement that the Sabbath is to preserve life speaks not only to its obvious celebrative, restorative function in enabling us to regroup emotionally and spiritually. His wider reference is to religion generally. Its purpose is to restore life at the deepest levels. It is in this light that the ascetic, penitential practices of the Church must be seen. They are meant to uncover those deep wells of spiritual energy within us that can be kept closed by the surface pleasures of hedonism.

Point

The deep spring of our emotional and psychological well-being is spiritual.

TUESDAY — Twenty-Third Week of the Year
1 Cor 6:1-11   *Lk 6:12-19*

First Reading

The Corinthians seem to have been an unusually litigious group of people. Their constant suing of one another in court was, to Paul, an indicator of a serious breakdown. He presents three reasons why they should refrain from such public displays of legal duelling. It is destructive of the Christian public image. Secondly, it points to an erosion of the reality of Christian love among them leaving it simply a rhetorical fancy. Disputes that inevitably arise should either be settled by the parties themselves or by a fellow-Christian as a binding arbitrator. Finally, this constant litigation is symptomatic of larger problems in the Church. Today, we take it for granted that Christians will sue each other. Few Catholics will have recourse to their pastor as an arbitrator and, in some cases, will even sue the pastor. The contentiousness that we take for granted raises serious questions as to what it means to live the Gospel in our world.

Gospel Reading

Just as Jesus prayed before He made His selection of Apostles, so prayer should precede the major decisions of our life. Conflicts among us will inevitably arise. It is no sign of maturity to paper them over with synthetic smiles. Our differences must be approached with candor and honesty. It is important, however, that we pray before we deal with conflict. Such prayer opens our minds to the work of the Holy Spirit, reminds us that there is a larger dimension at work in the world than a specific conflict, and encourages us to participate in advancing the kingdom of God even in our resolution of conflicts. The Lord's time of prayer had precisely these functions. It was a time when He let the Father's will inform His choices.

Point

Prayer will not bring an automatic solution to our conflicts for us. It will enable us to resolve them in a Christ-filled spirit.

WEDNESDAY — Twenty-Third Week of the Year
1 Cor 7:25-31   *Lk 6:20-26*

First Reading

The context in which Paul is writing is important to comprehend the full thrust of what he is saying in today's reading. These Corinthian letters come from a time when Paul believed the Lord's return to be imminent. For this reason, he advocates no change in life style among his readers. Because the time is short, they should not bother to marry or separate from their wives in dedication to the Lord. There is not enough time for such major changes because the world order is very quickly coming to a close. He is clear that these recommendations are his own opinion without any direct mandate from the Lord. Virginity can acquire other meanings when the world order is seen to be more stable. Virginity and celibacy send messages to our society. They remind our world that there is more to human fulfillment than sexual gratification. They are not a depreciation of marriage. Christian marriage sends its own message to the world. However, in a culture of promiscuity and easy virtue, the virgin and celibate are living reminders that the identity of a person can be expressed in many ways.

Gospel Reading

A stark contradictory challenge to popular values is also the message of today's Gospel reading. This section is from Luke's version of the Sermon on the Mount, sometimes called the "Sermon on the Plain." Luke's versions of the Beatitudes are abbreviated and less spiritualized than are those of Matthew. Luke is very much the evangelist to the outcast and the poor as well as to the upwardly mobile Gentiles who tended to forget those at the margins of society. His Gospel was written to assure the outcasts of a privileged place in the kingdom of God. Jesus assures the impoverished, hungry, hated and persecuted that society's evaluation of them is neither final nor definitive. They have a different place in God's scale. Society's evaluation of the wealthy and popular is also not final nor definitive. They, too, have a different location on God's scale.

Point

Individual fulfillment can take many forms.

THURSDAY — Twenty-Third Week of the Year
1 Cor 8:1-7, 11-13   *Lk 6:27-38*

First Reading

Let us describe, analyze and apply this problem of meat sacrificed to idols which Paul considers in today's first reading. Meat that had been brought to be offered to idols in Corinth became the property of the temple priests. After the day's sacrifices were over, the meat was sold to local butchers. Some Corinthian Christians joined their pagan friends for dinner which included some of this sacrificed meat. This raised the issue. Strict constructionists maintained that Christians' dining on this meat made them accomplices in the pagan ritual. The liberals were gorging themselves on this meat in the belief that because the pagan ritual was meaningless, any assertion of alleged quasi-participation was hot air. Paul agrees that the idols are meaningless and that this sacrificed meat is a lot of baloney. He made a prudential argument, however. Strangers who see Christians eating this "sacral meat" might be scandalized and confused. We can apply the same argument to astrology. Our excessive or playful reliance on it might cause weaker Christians to have their faith shaken. The point is that we must consider the effects of our conduct on others; we should be aware of their sensibilities. We cannot jam our spiritual insight down another person's throat.

Gospel Reading

This point finds broader expression in today's Gospel reading. It is Jesus' thoroughgoing indictment of narcissism and an extremely dramatic reminder to take others into consideration as we live out our lives. Christian life is not simply a religious version of everyday life. It is a different way of acting, thinking, playing, working, driving, investing, conversing and dealing with others. By the way we live, we create the kind of society that surrounds us.

Point

The measure we use will be used for us.

FRIDAY — Twenty-Third Week of the Year
1 Cor 9:16-19, 22-27   *Lk 6:39-42*

First Reading

In his dealing with several conflicts that plagued the Corinthian community, Paul is charged with inconsistency. He is accused of trying to be all things to all people. He admits that charge and turns it into a virtue. In one of his most vigorous self-defenses, he insists that he simply keeps his eye on the goal of preserving unity and bringing people to Christ. Let theologians worry about theoretical consistency; he has churches to run. Paul's passionate concern is to separate out the vital issues from the secondary ones. It is critical that this fledgling Christian community not bog down in a great many little disputes and lose their fundamental unity and sense of purpose. Paul insists that he keeps his eye on the "big picture." Somebody has to.

Gospel Reading

In today's Gospel reading, Jesus tells us that the blind cannot lead the blind. A leader must have vision and keep his eye on the goal and not be quick to judge. It is equally important for ourselves that we remember the "big picture" whether it be unity at home, work or parish. If we live alone, we can be as demanding as we wish. But when we live in a community, compromise is important. The issue that Paul has been tackling is the location of the dividing line between the negotiable and the non-negotiable. It is difficult at times to distinguish the trivial from the important. Everything in our life and in our religion is not at the same level. There is a hierarchy of values in our church life, spiritual life, work life, social life and personal life.

Point

Perspective, a gift of the Spirit, emerges out of experience and prayer.

SATURDAY — Twenty-Third Week of the Year
1 Cor 10:14-22   *Lk 6:43-49*

First Reading

The issue with which Paul deals in today's reading is Christian participation in idol worship. To do so was a logical extension of eating the meat sacrificed to idols. The liberal argument was logically flawless. If idolatry is bogus and idols are simply pieces of stone, there could be no harm in joining those services simply for social or professional reasons. The assumption was that informed Christians would know that pagan rites are a charade. Paul refuses so simplistic an argument. Participation in pagan rituals had a subtle influence. Gradually, by taking part in these cults, a person assimilates attitudes that its adherents share and begins to distance himself or herself either from the Christian assembly or the Christian mindset. The danger Paul sees is one of only partial immersion in the Christian mystery. A dabbling in pagan rites can lead to an embrace of a pluralistic potpourri of religious attitudes that would make Christianity either purely attitudinal or simply one more variant of a common religiosity.

Gospel Reading

The Lord speaks about the solid foundations of our life. If the foundation of our faith is the Lord Jesus, the foundation of our Christian life is discipleship—putting His words into practice. The Lord is stating that spiritual, mental or emotional adherence to the Gospel is not sufficient and will prove to be evanescent unless a person starts to slowly shape his or her discipleship into daily life. It is only by implementing our faith that we can test its seriousness, plumb its depths, chart its contours, see its cracks, discern its implications and discover its strength.

Point

Faith is not a dream or an emotion. It is a life to be lived.

MONDAY — Twenty-Fourth Week of the Year
1 Cor 11:17-26, 33   *Lk 7:1-10*

First Reading

This famous section of the letter to the Corinthians discloses some abuses at their liturgical eucharistic celebrations. It is a bit difficult to visualize the structure of these services. They probably were very similar to what we would call a church supper with the Eucharist celebrated at the conclusion. Rich and poor segments of the community gathered at a single celebration. It seems that the affluent came early and the poor came late. Paul remarks on the division of their celebration into cliques. He states that the very reason Jesus died was to bridge these separations and draw people together. Yet, the Corinthians were bringing the caste system of the marketplace into the Church. The point Paul is urging upon them is that Jesus gave us the Eucharist as a way to remember everything He did, said and taught about Christian love and community. The Corinthians were turning it into a way of reinforcing their factionalism.

Gospel Reading

Luke places great emphasis upon the universal scope of the Gospel message. The Roman centurion represents the Gentile world. Jesus responds to his request with the remark that such trust could not be discovered anywhere in Israel. The message of this incident for us is that the Lord Jesus is not the private possession of any one race, culture, ethnic group, nation or clique. Christ does not belong to us; we belong to Him. Jesus is not to be made into our image; we are to reflect Him. One way to grow into the likeness of the Lord is by a communal celebration of the Eucharist in the way that He intended.

Point

The meaning of Christian community should come alive, above all places, in our eucharistic celebrations.

TUESDAY — Twenty-Fourth Week of the Year
1 Cor 12:12-14, 27-31   *Lk 7:11-17*

First Reading

The Body of Christ in this world is unified but not homogeneous. Its many members are widely distributed and differently endowed. Such tremendous diversity can be held together only through the common Spirit of Christ. That single Spirit which we have all received in baptism links us together to make our various gifts, abilities, ministries and interests cohere into the single but pluriform continuation of the ministry of Jesus to our world. Such unity does not militate against hierarchy in the Church. Paul's ranking here is of special interest. Apostles are placed first followed by prophets: the ancient message and the message as applied. Teachers occupy a third position. They hand on the faith through instruction. They are followed by miracle workers, healers, helpers (a huge category), administrators and lastly those who speak in tongues. The ecstatic spiritual gifts follow those ministries that continue and sustain the daily operation of the church community.

Gospel Reading

The ministry of Jesus is seen at its most dramatic in His raising a dead boy to life and comforting a widow's grief. In doing so, Jesus *touched* the bier (cf. Numbers 19:11, where such an action causes ritual uncleanness). There are many ways of bringing new life to those who seem dead. Essentially, this is one way that the Church continues the work of Jesus. She tries to revive hope, faith and love in situations and among people that have forgotten the power of such virtues or think them to be merely childhood illusions. To the extent that the Church can exhibit the life and vitality of the Lord in her own ranks, she gives powerful witness to the fact that life is stronger than death and love is stronger than hate.

Point

The various ministries and gifts we share combine to breathe new life into our parish community.

WEDNESDAY — Twenty-Fourth Week of the Year
1 Cor 12:13-13:13　　　　　　　　　　　　　　*Lk 7:31-35*

First Reading

Paul's lyric to love seems to be almost an independent composition about the general virtue of love. Its placement in the letter to the Corinthians gives it an exact application and a very clear Christian reference. Paul is praising much more than love. He speaks of Christian love—the love shown to us by the Lord Jesus and the love we are commanded to express toward each other. The vices that took their toll on the Corinthian community were everything which Paul affirms love not to be. His central message in this magnificent poem is that religious observances without love are empty; ecstatic gifts are transient. What endures and enables a community to survive is love.

Gospel Reading

Paul's hymn to love cannot be divorced from the essential mystery that gives it life—the mystery of the cross. Paul's notion of agape derives from the self-sacrificing love of Jesus and not the romanticism of novels. This demanding notion of love is difficult for us to accept. The love on which the Lord insisted was never the slick emotion of our popular songwriting. The love which He summoned forth was much more deeply rooted in the will. It is no surprise that many found it difficult to accept His message and found rationalizations for refusing to receive His word. If the Baptist was far too ascetic to be followed, Jesus was too liberal to be a true Master. The Lord's final comment is that God's wisdom as He preached it is self-authenticating to all who accept it. In the same way, Paul's message of love is self-evident to those who make the decision to place their lives within the ambit of self-sacrificing love.

Point

We do not fall into Christian love. It derives from the call of Christ which we accept.

THURSDAY — Twenty-Fourth Week of the Year
1 Cor 15:1-11   *Lk 7:36-50*

First Reading

As Paul establishes his apostolic credentials in this first reading, he gives us one of the handful of absolutely critical sections of the New Testament. This is among the earliest testimonies to the Easter faith of the early Church. It is the first assertion in the New Testament that Jesus "died for our sins." This is a primal statement of the essence of the faith of the primitive apostolic community. These words link us to the faith of the early Church. Read and preached during the Easter season, they span the centuries to join the Church today with the fundamental event of Christianity—the Resurrection of the Lord.

Paul states that he became an Apostle out of the normal course—in an extraordinary way. He had not traveled with Jesus and did not have the credentials required of Matthias in the Acts of the Apostles. The central qualification upon which he relies is his vivid, direct and personal experience of the Risen Lord. That experience, as valid as that of the Eleven, was the enabling experience that allowed him to boast of the title of Apostle.

Gospel Reading

We cannot separate the teachings of saints and spiritual writers from the life experiences out of which they arise. Paul's powerful experience of Jesus' forgiveness drove home to him the transformative power of God's grace and the complete gift which forgiveness really is. This sets the background for today's Gospel reading. The woman who washes the feet of Jesus with her tears realizes not only her own sinfulness but also comes to experience the Lord's forgiveness. That combination creates saints and powerful apostles. A recognition of sin alone leads to spiritual pessimism. A recognition of God's willingness to forgive, by itself, can lead to cheap grace and automatic religion. When the crosshairs of repentance and forgiveness meet in our souls, saints are born.

Point

The experience of forgiven sin is the founding experience of the Christian life.

FRIDAY — Twenty-Fourth Week of the Year
1 Cor 15:12-20 *Lk 8:1-3*

First Reading

A final issue which Paul confronts in this letter is the denial by some Corinthian Christians that Jesus actually rose from the dead (or perhaps the belief that the Resurrection was limited to Jesus as a past event and is not a present reality among them). Paul is insistent that we are Christians not because we believe that Jesus died but because we believe that He rose from the grave. We are Christians not because we believe that people die, but because we believe that they will rise. The Resurrection of Christ is the single event from which everything else follows: our resurrection, forgiveness, new and eternal life. If we are joined to the Risen Lord in baptism, everything that happened to Him will happen to us. We are Christians, therefore, not because we believe in sin, death and suffering. That is not distinctive to us. A look around any neighborhood reveals those realities to anyone. We are Christians because we believe that reconciliation is possible, that death is actually the beginning of a different kind of life and that suffering has redeeming power.

Gospel Reading

In today's Gospel reading, Jesus is followed by several people he had cured, exorcised or enlivened. In a sense they represent the entire Christian movement, as all the people who have been touched by His saving power follow Him down through the ages. Just as Jesus moved about Galilee, so today His risen presence is a dynamic force within the material universe. Today, He continues the same ministry in a different way.

Point

Taken by itself, the passion of Jesus is a tragic story. Linked with the Resurrection, it becomes the story of the world's salvation. That was why the early Church remembered each of its details.

SATURDAY — Twenty-Fourth Week of the Year
1 Cor 15:35-37, 42-49   *Lk 8:4-15*

First Reading

Paul answers some questions about the mechanics of Resurrection. This is no metaphysical speculation in which he is engaging. Paul is trying to show that the Resurrection of Christ as well as the resurrection promised to all the baptized is not simply the reanimation of a corpse. It is instant transformation. Christ was not changed into a spook or a ghost. He entered a different kind of existence. Every part of Him was changed into a qualitatively different kind of life. The same is promised to us. This is the reason Paul dwells on the distinction between physical and spiritual bodies. As different as seed is from what grows from it, so will our risen life far exceed our life here. Paul strains the edges of language to articulate something that he intuits by faith. We will be changed! The mechanics of that change are not plain to us. What is clear is that what occurred to the Lord Jesus will take place with us.

Gospel Reading

The famous parable of the seed finds an appropriate place with this reading from Paul's letter. Paul had been at pains to explain how this earthly life is transformed into risen life. He could only describe it as a miraculous change. The same is true of the seed planted in good ground. Its change and result are miraculous. Although there are no eyewitnesses to the actual rising of Christ, we witness every day a kind of resurrection as the word of God takes shape in people's lives. How a brief reading of Scripture, a wafer of eucharistic bread, a few drops of baptismal water can create great movements, heroic saints and a torrent of spiritual insight remains a miracle. Every dimension of the Church today began with some individual's hearing the word of God and acting upon it. In more ways than one, the Church today is living proof of Jesus' Resurrection and the volcanic power of His Word in people's lives.

Point

The risen Lord shows Himself in His effect upon people in thousands of ways every day.

MONDAY — Twenty-Fifth Week of the Year
Pr 3:27-34   *Lk 8:16-18*

First Reading

The first readings for this week and next will be taken from some Old Testament Wisdom books. The Book of Proverbs is so named because it is packed with a great many disconnected proverbs. Each of them articulates a little piece of accumulated community wisdom of the "stitch in time . . ." variety. Most of them, surprisingly, make a great deal of sense to us so many centuries later. They are prescriptions for a life in solidarity with others, e.g., "Plot no evil against him who lives at peace with you." The Book of Proverbs is a grand illustration of the continuity of human nature. These proverbs, written several thousand years ago in a different culture with a different language, way of life and economy, remain true for us. Human beings across time and space have a great deal more in common than they have separating them.

Gospel Reading

We are familiar with Matthew's report of Jesus' saying that we should light a lamp for all to see. Luke, however, uses the Lord's words to make a different point. Jesus explains His parables and then makes this assertion about light. The light, in Luke, refers to the parables. They were ways of making Jesus' message about the kingdom clear in a way much more accurate, actually, than the conceptual. The parables are about ordinary people: fathers, widows, workers, housewives and rambunctious tenants. Through them the Lord shows the kingdom truths shining through ordinary human experience.

Point

The proverbs and parables show the religious dimension of ordinary experience.

TUESDAY — Twenty-Fifth Week of the Year
Pr 21:1-6, 10-13   *Lk 8:19-21*

First Reading

The loose collection of proverbs in today's first reading is more or less about justice. They are less about justice as an abstract ideal than they are about just living. "To do what is right and just is more acceptable to the Lord than sacrifice." Just living is enormously complex. The number of interests and causes that seek out our attention through the year is huge. Yet, we must find a way to balance our responsibilities to our family, fellow-Christians, and community at large. It is no virtue, for example, to devote great blocks of time to a parish with little time left for one's own children. Just living, accordingly, requires a constant re-examination of our priorities as well as how we regard the various people who want our time, money and assistance. We cannot completely fulfill all the requests made to us. That effort at balancing comprises the virtues of justice and prudence.

Gospel Reading

The Lord states that those who hear His words and keep them are as close to Him as His natural family. There is no reason to believe that Jesus did not have an extended family as virtually everyone did in those days. He announces in this Gospel reading that His true extended family is bound together by faith and works. Hearing the Lord's words and keeping them is a generic description. In the concrete case, we must each apply His words to our own life. Hearing the Gospel read in church is only an initial step. Applying its admonitions to our particular family life requires prayer and intelligence. After all, the Lord seeks not puppets but disciples.

Point

There is no prefabricated mold for the just life or the Christian life. In each case, it is a product of intelligent and prayerful decision.

WEDNESDAY — Twenty-Fifth Week of the Year
Pr 30:5-9   *Lk 9:1-6*

First Reading

This is the only prayer in the entire Book of Proverbs. It

prays for neither affluence nor poverty. If one becomes wealthy, he or she can easily forget God. If a person is ridden with poverty, he or she will be forced to steal and so turn from God. It is a prayer for balance. More deeply, however, it is a prayer to enable us to keep God as the real focus of our life. Both the things we have and do not have can so occupy the center of our attention that we forget the full meaning of our passage here on earth. We can come to define ourselves by the number of our possessions or depreciate our real worth because of the things we do not have.

Gospel Reading

Luke's version of Jesus' missionary instructions was intended for the early Church. The Lord instructs His disciples to preach and to cure diseases. The kingdom was not to be an exclusively spiritual enterprise but an event that renews people in body and in spirit. This has been the justification for the mammoth social apostolate of the Church. The instruction to travel without encumbrance places emphasis upon the Gospel as the rationale for the Church's existence. The more encumbrances we have, the more time and money become diverted into maintaining them rather than the message. This Gospel reading challenges us to find our identity first of all in our relationship with Christ rather than in the things we own or the income we can command. That relationship with Jesus defines, on the most profound level, who we are and what we are worth. The next step is to translate that self-definition into our life style.

Point

Holiness is not only for hermits and angels. Discipleship is intended, by the Lord, to take place inside this world.

THURSDAY — Twenty-Fifth Week of the Year
Ec 1:2-11   *Lk 9:7-9*

First Reading

The Book of Ecclesiastes, sometimes called *Qoheleth*, is part of the Wisdom literature. Its theme is captured in the first verse: everything is vanity—exhaled and empty air. Everything seems to be pointless as life moves in cycles. Tomorrow will be the same as yesterday. Everything is already decided. Nothing we can do can give it any other meaning. If there is meaning to this vast endless cycle of events, it remains hidden to us. Why was Ecclesiastes so pessimistic? One reason may be the times in which it was composed. The great creative period of Israel's history was over. The Jewish people had lost the sense of God speaking to them through the events of history. Here, in exile, God's voice was silent. Ecclesiastes makes no reference to covenant, exodus or deliverance. History had lost its power as revelation. The people turned to the world of nature to see something of God. There, they discovered only the great cosmic cycles of the seasons, years and days. Although we might not share Ecclesiastes' pessimism, it is a lesson in humility for us in that we cannot, in this life, comprehend the full significance of all that occurs in our lives.

Gospel Reading

In the New Testament, especially Luke's Gospel, we have a different atmosphere from Ecclesiastes. In the New Testament, events are loaded with meaning. God speaks through natural history, world history, Church history and our personal history. We are in an atmosphere that is decidedly non-cyclical. In today's Gospel reading, Herod looks for the meaning of Jesus. The Gospel writers saw meaning packed into every event and gesture of the Lord's earthly life. Here, in Jesus, God is on the offensive. In this era, we are moving rapidly from promise to fulfillment much as did the Israelites in the exodus. In the period of the Church, we have sacraments and signs of the Lord's inviting and driving presence. We can indeed see God in the world of nature as did Ecclesiastes. We can also see the Lord speaking to us and calling us forward as a Church, as a parish and as individuals.

Point

The assumption of the Christian faith is that we are not on a cosmic merry-go-round. The Lord is leading us forward to the kingdom and we will take very many people along with us.

FRIDAY — Twenty-Fifth Week of the Year
Ec 3:1-11   Lk 9:18-22

First Reading

These readings show a principal difference between Ecclesiastes and Luke. This famous passage describes the great circle of time: "Turn, turn, turn." Everything has its time and season. We experience these times but cannot understand why they happen or if they have any directedness. Their meaning, shape or content seem to forever elude our grasp. All we are able to do is to submit to the brute cycle of life. We cannot pierce through the cycle to discover its meaning. All we can see is the cycle. Human life is only eternal return. This sums up the Book of Ecclesiastes.

Gospel Reading

In today's Gospel reading, we have a different rhythm to life than that of Ecclesiastes. In Jesus' prediction of the suffering,

dying and rising of the Messiah, we have the basic structure of
Christian life. It is a rhythm with a destination, however. We are
not cogs in some gigantic mechanical wheel of fate that grinds
on slowly and unavoidably. We make choices, take chances,
sign contracts and fill our lives with decisions. We can turn our
episodes of suffering and dying into the building blocks of a
closer life with the Lord which is synonymous with Resurrection life. All we have done with our lives will be taken up and
made forever part of us in the final resurrection. Through the
Resurrection of Christ, we can pierce through the cycle of time
to see the meaning and destination of our suffering and joys: a
risen, dynamic life with the Lord.

Point

*Trying to assimilate ourselves to Christ in every particular
of our life gives significance to the entire trajectory of a lifetime.*

SATURDAY — Twenty-Fifth Week of the Year
Ec 11:9-12:8   Lk 9:43-45

First Reading

This is an enigmatic section of Ecclesiastes. His message
seems to be that we should savor the joys of youth because they
will soon end. His description of the waning days of life is
somber and depressing. His point is that we should not only
remember the vigor of youth as a happy memory but also recall
the vigor of a young person's faith. The passage of years tempts
that faith, hardens hearts, and leaves a person alone and befud-
dled before the mystery of life, anxious to return to the dust. The
dust returns to the earth and the breath of life returns to the God
who gave it. There is no clear view here of any kind of life after
death. A reflective reading of this passage will spotlight for us

the great gift of the Resurrection and the hope that the promise of eternal life gives to us. This reading throws us back to a time when the eternal life we take for granted was generally not understood by the Hebrews. That absence of hope in eternal life deprived life on earth of any lasting significance.

Gospel Reading

The Gospels can emphasize and celebrate the suffering of the Lord because they were written in the light of His Resurrection. To the disciples, the prospect of suffering was catastrophic. They thought that the Messiah's suffering and death indicated that the promised kingdom was a temporary fantasy. With the Resurrection of Jesus, a thoroughly new dimension to life here and to the mission of the Church was released. It was as though the Lord had discovered a brand new continent that nobody knew existed and which suddenly made sense of all the gaps in the old maps. The hope of this eternal life can now give meaning to suffering, pain and death by making them vehicles of an everlasting glory.

Point

The hope of eternal life does not leave our life here unchanged. It transforms its meaning.

MONDAY — Twenty-Sixth Week of the Year
Jb 1:6-22   *Lk 9:46-50*

First Reading

This week, we consider the story of Job. Written about 600 years before Christ, the Book of Job is the longest sustained piece of Hebrew poetry or drama we have. Possibly, there was a man named Job whose story was told and retold until it became a legend and was recounted as such. The opening scene of a heavenly conspiracy in today's first reading indicates the heavy stylization of this story. The Book of Job is less a story of suffering (as it is usually interpreted to be) than it is a story of faith. A point that should be highlighted is that it takes place in Uz (Syria) which indicates that Job, the Bible's great man of long-suffering faith, was a Gentile.

Gospel Reading

Jesus says that whoever is not against us is on our side. He reminds us that there are many people of good faith like Job who have dedicated their lives to relieving human suffering and are moved by the Spirit of God as best they can perceive Him. They work outside the formal boundaries of the Catholic Church. The Red Cross, Alcoholics Anonymous, Special Olympics programs and community groups come to mind. Many people in such groups serve a God they cannot name and are moved by a Spirit they do not know. Their work is somehow connected to the victory of Jesus over evil. We can give that God a name and know that Spirit to be a Person. We express, ritualize and celebrate what these people of good will experience in an inchoate way. The Gospel they live out anonymously, we can loudly proclaim.

Point

In working to bring about the kingdom, we are surrounded by hundreds of natural allies.

TUESDAY — Twenty-Sixth Week of the Year
Jb 3:1-3, 11-17, 20-23   *Lk 9:51-56*

First Reading

We continue the masterful story of Job. After a series of

disasters had befallen this just man, he now sits on a dung heap in stunned silence. Finally, he utters a lament in which he curses not God, but the day of his birth. "Why, why, why?" is a question we have often asked, as did Judah in her exile. There is more going on in this Job story than meets the eye. The Book of Job is part of the Wisdom tradition, written during the exile. During that time of national torment and self-examination, the people of Judah were asking these same questions. They had kept the rules and the covenant most of the time and could not understand why this national tragedy was happening to them. They felt that their never having been born was preferable to a life in an emotional and national limbo.

Gospel Reading

This is a turning point in Luke's Gospel. Jesus is now set to go toward Jerusalem, the place of His suffering and of His glory. In the next several weeks, we will watch events unwind. This Gospel reading adds a significant dimension to Job's question. If our hope were limited to this world, if the meaning of everything we do must be verified in this life, then we are set for disappointment. If we search for complete justice, perfect equity, total fulfillment, complete happiness in this life, then suffering is more than a problem—it is a catastrophe. Jesus' Resurrection tells us that there is more, a great deal more. His Resurrection gives us a wide angle lens. Justice, equity, fulfillment and happiness might start here, but we can be absolutely certain that they will endure and be completed in God's presence. The proof of this is the Resurrection of Jesus.

Point

We celebrate the Eucharist through difficult times so that we can sustain ourselves in the power of the promise of Easter.

WEDNESDAY — Twenty-Sixth Week of the Year
Jb 9:1-12, 14-16   *Lk 9:57-62*

First Reading

After Job's lament over the disaster that befell him, his friends come by to console him. They present the standard theological explanation for his problems. The causality in the universe is strict. God rewards the good and punishes evil. Therefore, Job must have done wrong and sinned somewhere, sometime in the past. Where there is smoke, there is fire. This was the conventional wisdom against which the Book of Job protests. The problem with so facile an explanation is that it places God into a box. He becomes an insurer of success much like a cosmic vending machine into which we put our good works to get our reward. It really makes God into our image and likeness. We know that every suffering is not a punishment. That is the error of the theology of Job's friends. The Book of Job insists on God's sovereign majesty and mystery to which we can only submit.

Gospel Reading

If suffering were God's punishment for sin, it would be difficult to understand why Jesus and His disciples were tormented, persecuted, hunted and killed. The presence of suffering in our world says more about the world than it does about God. What we do know is that the God of this immense universe was suddenly nailed down on wooden crossbars outside the walls of old Jerusalem, like a criminal. If we can span that distance between Genesis and Calvary, then we will begin to approach the mystery and majesty of God's love.

Point

We cannot box the God of Easter into a mechanical formula.

THURSDAY — Twenty-Sixth Week of the Year
Jb 19:21-27   *Lk 10:1-12*

First Reading

The Job story is a drama in several acts. Job personifies Judah in exile seeking answers to the enigma of innocent suffering. Job hits upon an insight so important that he wishes that his words were written down somewhere. If God does not speak now, He will at some future time. This is one of the few hints in the Old Testament of immortality and eternal life. It is a picture of mankind begging for resurrection. It is the beginning of an answer that there must be an eternity to balance things out. We see the first approximation of a conclusion to which Job gradually comes. In God's time all will be made right.

Gospel Reading

Jesus counsels us against too superficial a judgment about the success of the Gospel, prayer or the Church. There is a recalcitrance built into human nature that is not easily eradicated. The reception of God's grace is necessary to open people's hearts to the Lord's healing power. The Lord Jesus assures His disciples that there is an accounting. Beyond the various measures of success and failure we adopt in this world, there will come a moment when the Lord will apply His measure of success or failure. It is a standard exposed to world view on Calvary. It is neither financial nor numerical. It is obedience to God's word. Jesus asks His disciples that they simply obey the Father's will. The rest is in the hands of God.

Point

The full story of what we have done with our life and love is never fully told in this life.

FRIDAY — Twenty-Sixth Week of the Year
Jb 38:1, 12-21; 40:3-5   *Lk 10:13-16*

First Reading

God now speaks to Job out of the tempest (or the "whirl-wind" in older translations). It is a description of Job's experi-ence of God. He is overwhelmed with God's majesty and power. "I am God. You are man." It is clear that God will not talk with him as an equal. There follows some of the most magnificent poetry ever written. "Have you ever commanded the morning . . . have you entered the sources of the sea?" God tells Job that human beings cannot completely discern the mystery of life. They should have faith in God's providence. Period!

Such an answer leaves us unsatisfied. The Wisdom tradi-tion has a strand, of which Job and Ecclesiastes are part, which affirms that although life has a meaning, we cannot know it. This image of God is overwhelming and, though true, only partial. They did not perceive God as Father.

Gospel Reading

In today's reading, the Lord makes two central affirma-tions. The first is that the divine Word is available now not in the majestic whirlwind but in the preaching of the disciples. The message of eternal life that we have in Jesus is to be transmitted through His followers. The second powerful affir-mation is that the judgment on the impenitent towns is a self-imposed sentence. The final judgment of our eternal des-tiny is not arbitrary and capricious. Jesus has given us the key to eternal life: hear His words and keep them. We no longer ignorantly cower before the inscrutable majesty of God. He has told us all we need to know about eternal life and its acquisition through His Son, Jesus. If God showed Himself to be a God of power in the Job story, He shows Himself to be a God of suffering love in Jesus.

Point

Job experienced God in the whirlwind. We experience God in the crucified love of Jesus.

SATURDAY — Twenty-Sixth Week of the Year
Jb 42:1-3, 5-6, 12-16   *Lk 10:17-24*

First Reading

The Job story has a happy ending. Everything he lost comes back double. God was pleased with Job. But now Job is a different person. He has come to know the living God. Before, he knew God by hearsay and tradition. The answers to life's problems were those that had been handed to him. Out of his personal struggle, he wrought a personal faith. The glib answers were gone and he came to see that God is larger than our conceptions of Him. We cannot impose our ways of doing business on Him. God is not here to fulfill our expectations.

We can expand that point to say that the spiritual domain is a mystery. We try to approach it with theology, liturgy and ritual. But God's Spirit, grace and will operate as and where they will. We cannot control but only acknowledge and submit to the mystery of God.

Gospel Reading

The Lord Jesus tells His disciples about the power of His name. Snakes and scorpions will do them no harm. The preaching of the Gospel will change their lives and transform personalities. The power of the Gospel remains a mystery even to the Church. We cannot catalogue and systematize the reach of the Holy Spirit. All we are able to do is acknowledge the magnificent apostolate and treasure given us as we try to become worthy of it. There is much more at work in our world, our Church and lives than what we are able to see. Amid all of our structures and efforts is the power of the Holy Spirit slowly moving and weaving events and hearts together.

Point

Father, Son and Spirit are a mystery that dwells not in outer space but beneath all reality. Our access to that very real dimension, which upholds all we can see, is through faith.

MONDAY — Twenty-Seventh Week of the Year
Gal 1:6-12   Lk 10:25-37

First Reading

Paul's letter to the Galatians is one of the most important letters of the New Testament both as to the biographical information it contains about Paul and as a product of the hot debates that surrounded the Church's emergence out of Judaism. Initially, the early Christians viewed themselves as a saving remnant within Judaism. For a variety of reasons, the Church began to see itself as increasingly independent of Jewish institutions much as the earth was spun out of the sun. At the time Paul wrote this letter, the Christian community was half in and half out of Judaism. The debate centered on the requirements for admission of Gentiles into the Church. The conservative wing saw the Church as yet part of Judaism and sought to impose the requirement of circumcision on all. The liberal wing, of which Paul was a part, saw the Church as distinct from Judaism with the requirement of circumcision supplanted by faith in the Lord Jesus. In this first reading, we can detect the passion that attached to this issue. Paul is astonished that his converts were turning to some quasi-Jewish brand of Christianity. The issue that fired Paul's soul and pen was not hatred for the synagogue but the adequacy of what Christ had done on the cross.

Gospel Reading

The parable of the Good Samaritan enables many points to be made. The punch line of the story might be lost on us. Its effect today would be as if Jesus concluded the story with the statement that the one who had helped the beaten man was a member of the PLO! One could hear a Jewish audience reacting. The point of the parable is that love is not calculating. It meets human need as it finds it. Secondly, status is not the guarantee of salvation. It is the good we do that ultimately counts. This is the point Paul seeks to make in his assertion that faith is more important than ritual circumcision.

The parables are usually stated in extreme terms to drive home a point while reminding us that we all fall short of perfection to cut off any claim to be self-righteous. Exclusive reliance on circumcision as an assurance of salvation could have precisely that effect.

Point

The true mark of membership in God's people is not physical.

TUESDAY — Twenty-Seventh Week of the Year
Gal 1:13-24   *Lk 10:38-42*

First Reading

The letter to the Galatians is among the earlier writings of

Paul. It outlines some of the great themes of his theology that will receive more elaborate and dispassionate presentation in the letter to the Romans. Galatians is a kind of first draft written in the heat of battle. As Paul writes this letter, his blood pressure is sky-high. In today's reading, he is defending both what he preached and his right to preach it against certain agitators who pervaded the Galatian Christian community. He states that he was called to the specific task of bringing the Gospel to Gentiles. He was not one more of many teachers but an Apostle commissioned directly by the Lord. Although he was not among the original Twelve, his mission is from the same Lord. He is very clear that he is preaching the Gospel and not simply another opinion.

Gospel Reading

The parable of the Good Samaritan focused on the importance of good works. Luke now explains the importance of hearing and studying the Word of God as well. In this little Gospel vignette, Martha represents the doing while Mary symbolizes the hearing. Jesus stresses the importance of listening to the Word of God. Hearing God's Word and the study of doctrine are important because they shape and guide our expressions of faith and love. Church doctrine is not a luxury. It helps us to put our faith, hope and love into words, to share it with others and to help define who we are as Christians. Doctrine assists us in understanding why we do what we do. It enables us to integrate our faith with the broader intellectual world-view we have learned from our culture. Doctrine enables us to see how what we believe "fits" into everything else we know. This is the reason for Paul's insistence on his Gospel as correct and authentic.

Point

A deeper understanding of God's word and the teaching of

our Church should deepen our knowledge and love of the Lord Jesus.

WEDNESDAY — Twenty-Seventh Week of the Year
Gal 2:1-2, 7-14   *Lk 11:1-4*

First Reading

The first reading describes Paul's version of the Council of Jerusalem and bears interesting comparison with Luke's account in Acts 15. Several notable things emerge from Paul's recollection of events. First, Paul defends his ministry by insisting that he was in accord with the pillars of the Church in Jerusalem. Harmony with the Jerusalem Church was an indicator of continuity with the apostolic tradition. In the second place, Paul affirms his equality with the pillar Apostles but not his independence of them. Thirdly, Paul views it as important that he disagreed with Cephas whom he names without further introduction indicating a common knowledge of Peter's significance. Peter probably played the role of conciliator in the heated discussion. Paul, driven on this issue of Jewish practices, disagreed with Peter's conciliating behavior. Finally, Paul nowhere mentions the "decree" of the Jerusalem council. This episode indicates the importance of Peter, the passion of this issue and the role of a central authenticating Church.

Gospel Reading

Luke's version of the Lord's Prayer is more elliptical than the one given in Matthew's Gospel. Individual prayer is very much a personal activity. Its forms are various: centering prayer, meditation, the Rosary, biblical prayer, shared prayer, novena prayer, public prayer, litanic prayer, liturgical prayer, etc. What the Lord Jesus describes in these few words is an

attitude of prayer, a way of approaching God that was His own
and should therefore belong to every Christian. The exact
words themselves are secondary to the attitude they embody.
To the extent that we can assimilate the attitude of Jesus at
prayer, our prayer becomes as energizing and power-filled as
was His. Prayer is primarily a time to let the energy and power
of God flow through us. It should not become a duty but a time
for refreshment and invigoration.

It is important as well to recall that in prayer we are not
alone with God. We pray in union with the Church around the
world. As Paul shows in today's first reading, the spiritual unity
that binds us together is more important than the particular
practices and expressions we use.

Point

*We are joined together as a Church less by the fact that we
pray in exactly the same way as by the fact that we pray to the
same Lord.*

THURSDAY — Twenty-Seventh Week of the Year
Gal 3:1-5   *Lk 11:5-13*

First Reading

After Paul had defended his apostolic credentials, he pro-
ceeds to defend the Gospel he preaches. The people who were
attacking Paul allowed Gentiles to enter the Church only after
fulfilling Jewish entry requirements. The entrants needed to be
circumcised. This was no secondary issue when adults were
seeking to become Christians. Paul opposed this vehemently
by arguing that if circumcision were necessary to become a
Christian, Christ's death was useless. We are either saved by
faith in Christ or not at all. Since Jesus came, the Law, we
realize, is powerless to save. We do not earn salvation. It is a

gift. It is a transformation given to us by the power of grace. Paul sees it as a great disaster that the Galatians who began in faith would thereby end in the flesh—that is, in the Jewish signs of salvation: kosher table and circumcision. The Law is a useful assist in living our faith but it is not an independent source of salvation. This sharp statement of Paul's position explains why the letter to the Galatians has been called the Magna Carta of Christian liberty.

Gospel Reading

Jesus speaks about faith and prayer. It is not the words we use but the faith with which we say them that is important. The precise point of the Lord's parable is crucial here. He does not compare the Father to a reluctant parent from whom we have to extract an answer to our prayer. Rather, Jesus uses a rabbinic form of argument from the lesser to the greater. For example, if a child can do something, how much more can an adult do so; if a priest can perform a ritual, how much more can the Pope do so; if voluntary prayer is forbidden in schools, how much more is mandatory prayer disallowed. If a reluctant man responds to repeated requests, how much more will God. The Lord encourages us to pray with faith. The quality of our prayer is more important than its quantity.

Point

Our prayer should be quality time with God.

FRIDAY — Twenty-Seventh Week of the Year
Gal 3:7-14   *Lk 11:15-26*

First Reading

Paul's argument with the Judaizers continues. The issue of

circumcision was only the tip of the iceberg. It was, in fact, a way to reinstall all the old religious machinery of Judaism into Christianity through the back door. This is the reason for Paul's emphatic assertion that faith saves and not circumcision. The question here cannot be simply stated as faith in the heart (which is good) as opposed to religious ritual (which is bad). That is not the issue. There are really two views of religion at war here. One view sees religion as working automatically. To be circumcised is to be a son of Abraham and heir to the promise. Salvation comes from membership in the chosen people. The other view, which is Paul's, is that religion primarily gives expression to faith. All rituals, including circumcision, are expressions of faith. The life-giving personal relationship to Christ is the only trigger of salvation. It opens the way for His life, light and power to flow into us. If there is no faith, any ritual is meaningless for us. Paul had no special animus against circumcision as ritual. His fight was against circumcision as an independent, autonomous, self-sufficient guarantee of salvation.

Gospel Reading

The readings refer to external cleanliness and ritual purity. Holiness must be interiorized. If a house is clean but the family within is riddled with self-righteousness and arrogance, such a family is worse off because the condition of their house gives them false illusions. There is a constant temptation to make religion automatic. The problem of personal change is too difficult and has little of the excitement of exorcisms. It is very easy to search out automatic things: blessings, rituals, purifications that will do the work for us and wash us over by making us holy. The sacraments and rituals of the Church are infallible channels of God's availability to us. But they operate upon us only to the extent of our faith. The more profound a person's faith, the deeper will be his or her sacramental encounter with the Lord.

Point

The power, love and glory of the Lord are available to us through sacramental faith.

SATURDAY — Twenty-Seventh Week of the Year
Gal 3:22-29
                                                              Lk 11:27-28

First Reading

Paul begins a discussion about the function of the Old Law and of law in general for the Christian. Not only is he discussing two testaments but two stages of spiritual development in every individual as well. Under the Old Law, the sanction of sin was necessary to teach people to obey the covenant through external controls. The Law served as a guide much as the rules of our parents and schools guided virtually every item of our behavior as children. With the coming of Christ and the infusion of His Spirit into our hearts, we have an internal Governor, as it were, Who enables us slowly to put on the mind of Christ. We are motivated less by constraint than we are impelled by the love for and from Christ in us. In the same way, as children mature, the need for detailed regulations recedes as they internalize the rules and come to see the wisdom of restraints that until now had been imposed. The index of a mature adult is the ability to live responsibly without referring to the presence or absence of rules. The index of spiritual maturity is the shift of focus in our spiritual lives from law to God's presence.

Gospel Reading

Our obedience to the Word of God and its implementation in our lives is our point of resemblance to the Lord Jesus. This is a stronger bond to Christ than the biological bonds of family. We are like the Lord not because we share the same biochemical composition, physical features, language or genetic inheritance. We are most like Jesus when we place our lives into the Father's hands as He did.

Point

Law is the beginning but not the end of spiritual adulthood.

MONDAY — Twenty-Eighth Week of the Year
Gal 4:22-24, 26-27, 31-5:1   *Lk 11:29-32*

First Reading

We have two Old Testament references in today's readings: one by Paul and the other by Jesus. Paul recalls the story of Abraham and the promise. Sarah was old and past the age of childbearing. She suggested that Abraham take the slave girl Hagar as a surrogate mother. Hagar gave birth to Ishmael while Sarah later gave birth to Isaac, the child of the promise. Paul uses a curious rabbinic style of allegory to assert that the slave Hagar represented the Law and the old covenant. Sarah was the free woman through whom the child of promise was born. As such she represents the new covenant. Paul uses this allegory to urge the Galatians not to revert to a religion of law that makes them afraid of their own shadows, bound like little children. Only through the freedom given them in Christ can they expand into spiritual adults and let all the Old Testament promises come true through them.

Gospel Reading

The people continue to seek a miracle. Jesus responds that the only sign they will receive is the sign of Jonah. In the context of Luke's Gospel, the sign of Jonah has a special meaning. We often think of the fish that swallowed Jonah for three days and later spit him upon the shore to resume his journey to the place where God wanted him to prophesy. But when Jonah did prophesy (unwillingly) in Nineveh, the surprising thing was that the people immediately took his message to heart. By using this reference, the Lord is effectively saying that the Jonah sign and miracle that should prove convincing is that people are listening to the Word of God and allowing it to take effect in their lives. Their experience of the Holy Spirit is the great and powerful sign. To see such an event as a miracle takes faith. This free response to the Gospel message is the great sign that the Holy Spirit is at work in people's lives.

Point

The purpose of religion is not to impose a crushing burden upon people or to turn life into an obstacle course. Its purpose is to fill us with the power of God so we can more fully live our lives.

TUESDAY — Twenty-Eighth Week of the Year
Gal 5:1-6 *Lk 11:37-41*

First Reading

Paul continues his passionate argument that faith and not the Law is what saves us. He tells the Galatians that their reception of circumcision binds them to the entire Law and all the other old covenant rituals. Yet, after Jesus rose from the grave, these very rituals will no longer do them any good. More important than ritual observances is a faith which knows the Lord Jesus personally. Paul is speaking here of faith not as doctrine but as personal self-entrustment to the Lord. This personal relationship with Christ replaces the Law and is forged through the Holy Spirit at work in our hearts. Paul's passion on this point is very strong, to the point of poor taste and lack of charity. He adds in verse twelve of this chapter that if these Judaizers are so devoted to circumcising others, let their knife slip so they will castrate themselves. For Paul and the early Church this was a hot issue.

Gospel Reading

We have a dinner party that turned into a disaster. A Pharisee had invited Jesus to a meal and said the wrong thing. This caused the Lord to explode. Luke gives us a long series of denunciations not so much of individual Pharisees as of a Pharisaism that emphasized rituals over faith. The Pharisee's remark at Jesus' ceremonial negligence was the spark that ignited this classic diatribe. We can guess at the reasons for the Lord's severity. A religion reduced to externals becomes phony because it misdirects faith, hope and love. A person can be more in love with a romanticized version of "Catholicism" than with the actual community Jesus founded, more devoted to Church structure than to the people of the Church thereby turning the Church (or Judaism) into an idol. The result is that the love of Christ, the very soul of liturgy, parish and prayer, is stunted and misapplied to a fantasy of an idealized religiosity.

Point

Church laws and ecclesiastical conventions are vehicles of the Holy Spirit and should not be obstacles to Him.

WEDNESDAY — Twenty-Eighth Week of the Year
Gal 5:18-25   *Lk 11:42-46*

First Reading

We come to the end of the Galatian letter. Two points

need to be made. The word "flesh" in Paul's letters has a specific technical meaning. It refers to the entire physical and psychological structure of an individual without the Holy Spirit. Without the Spirit, a person is, for Paul, a "corpse." The "flesh" refers to the self-destructive centrifugal forces spinning us away from God. "Flesh," "old man," "carnal man" are all synonyms for a person without God. It is not an indictment of the human body as evil. Secondly, Paul's references to liberty in the Galatian letter are not synonymous with license. He speaks specifically of freedom from the ritual requirements of the Old Testament Law.

Throughout this letter, Paul had spoken of the shift from obedience to external law toward the internal government of the Holy Spirit. The Old Law could not enable an individual to obey itself. People broke the Law and in that very act became more aware of their sinfulness only to continue breaking the Law. It was very much like a dog chasing its own tail. Now, Paul insists, the Holy Spirit has broken that cycle and given us the power to overcome the centrifugal forces in us through His presence inside us. In place of the "old, carnal man" we have become a new creation. It is our lifelong task as Christians to yield to that inner power. So ends Galatians.

Gospel Reading

The dinner party continues to go to pieces. Jesus deprecates the Pharisees' insistence on tithing grain, fruit and even garden plants with extreme meticulousness while they neglect justice and love. Their spiritual energies are misdirected. A lawyer interrupts Jesus to suggest that He is speaking in such sweeping generalizations that some people might think that He is referring to the lawyers as well. Jesus turns on him to say, "Woe to you lawyers!" They laid an increasing number of burdens on people, snowballing religious conventions, expanding simple laws and placing their byzantine interpretations on the same level as revelation.

Point

There are hierarchies of truths and traditions. It is important to go back to the well in prayer to regain perspective.

THURSDAY — Twenty-Eighth Week of the Year
Ep 1:3-10   *Lk 11:47-54*

First Reading

We begin the letter to the Ephesians. After considering the problems that faced the Corinthian Church (incest and factions) and the tensions within the Galatian community that attached to the issue of circumcision, we stop now and soar among the clouds for a while. In this letter we look at the Church not from the bottom up but from Jesus' point of view. Ephesians is a sublime epistle. Its language and concepts are exalted. It reveals an overview of what the Christian experience is all about. It may have been from Paul himself or a disciple of his. Whichever is the case, it remains a letter written under the Holy Spirit. In a world where people, families, communities and churches are divided and torn apart, Ephesians reminds us that God's plan is to unite all things in Christ. The agent of this world-wide unification is to be the Church. To draw all things together under Christ is the mystery and design of God. Personal and societal dislocation, however caused, is a deviation from that plan.

Gospel Reading

The Pharisee dinner party continues to fall apart. It is important that we recall that the Pharisees were not completely corrupt. If they had been, their excesses would not be a lesson for us. Rather, they failed to differentiate their interpretations of law. It was a uni-dimensional approach to religion without nuance. It would be similar to our equation of Church law with divine law. The Pharisees have come to represent for us the tendency to turn means into ends in themselves. The mechanisms, specifics and legalities of Church life are not trivial. We do need, now and then, to sweep them up into the larger perspective of Ephesians as we remind ourselves that we are after all a Church with a divine mandate. Everything of us must be subsidiary to that goal.

Point

It is an exalted and frightening realization that to the people around us we are the commissioned agents of Christ.

FRIDAY — Twenty-Eighth Week of the Year
Ep 1:11-14   *Lk 12:1-7*

First Reading

The letter to the Ephesians explains its vision of unity within the Church as though the Church were a microcosm of the unity intended for all creation. "Us" and "you" refer to Jews and Gentiles. The Holy Spirit of unity that we share and experience is the proof, down payment, security deposit and first installment that God does actually plan to bring all people together in Christ. The Spirit we are able to experience now is proof that this vision of the unity of the human family is not simply rhetoric or an illusion. God's design is as real and workable as is the Church. In our time, the fact that a unified and diverse Catholic Church exists is assurance that a unified and diverse family of mankind is possible.

Gospel Reading

Jesus cautions His disciples to be wary of the hypocrisy of

the Pharisees. Such synthetic religiosity cannot be hidden forever. Like yeast, it will show itself sooner or later. Such theatrical religion cannot save, transform or give meaning to suffering. Our relationship to God is the most serious relation of our life and not a game. This is the sense in which we are told to fear the Lord. We know that God's will shall be accomplished in one way or another. He is not deceived by those who go through the motions and language of religion. We can fool a pastor, bishop or Pope; we cannot deceive the Lord.

Our interpretations of this Gospel passage will vary. That God sees into our hearts can be a source of magnificent comfort with the realization that despite our imperfection, He sees our true motives. It can also be a source of great terror if the public honors us as incarnating a holy ideal and all the while we know that God sees right through our image to the real state of affairs within our heart.

Point

This is God's judgment: We will live with our real self for eternity!

SATURDAY — Twenty-Eighth Week of the Year
Ep 1:15-23   *Lk 12:8-12*

First Reading

Paul gives us an exalted and thrilling vision of the place of the Christian in the Church. We are members of the Church under the headship of Christ. Our membership is not simply a superficial attachment to a self-functioning and autonomous organization. As members, we participate and share in that light and life of Christ that floods the Church. Each of us is an integral part of that community without whom the Church is diminished and with whom it can flourish even more. This is the reason Paul prays for a deepening of each Christian's inner sight to realize the transcendent vocation to which we are called. The more conscious each of us is of our role in the Church, of God's work through us and of our place in history, to that extent the entire Church has a more heightened awareness of its own ministry and role in the world. All insight is not confined to any one segment of the Church. The glorious inheritance is distributed among all the members of Christ's Body. This awareness of our baptismal calling makes us more effective members of the community of Jesus.

Gospel Reading

To refuse our inner vision, our spiritual insight, is a sin against the Holy Spirit. Jesus' strong words in today's Gospel reading remind us that the Holy Spirit has been given to each of us as Christians to enable us to actuate all the gifts given us for our mission in this life. The Holy Spirit enables us to know when to speak and when to remain silent. A denial of that spiritual light within us or a refusal to allow it to penetrate the conscious level of our awareness is a sin against the Spirit. The situation is analogous to a Christian who refuses the Eucharist, penance or an opportunity to pray. It is a self-contradiction. The Spirit has been given us as an integral part of ourselves to propel us toward maturity in the Lord.

Point

Each of us has received the Holy Spirit to live and to thrive as that Spirit gives us the light.

MONDAY — Twenty-Ninth Week of the Year

Ep 2:1-10   *Lk 12:13-21*

First Reading

The letter to the Ephesians draws several contrasts in today's first reading. There is the contrast between the psychological and spiritual death that sin entails and the life that flows from grace. There is the rebellious cosmic spirit that pervades the world and the spirit of obedience to God that is equally cosmic and penetrating. There is the contrast between our rebellion and the gift of love to us in Christ. Paul is speaking from his conversion experience. Only in hindsight can we recognize the rebellious, sinful ways that held us in thrall. The more accurately we view our past, the more gifted does our salvation in Jesus appear.

It is only when we have experienced salvation in Christ that we can place our loves, our world and our values into some kind of perspective. Just as a person who has stopped smoking can look back with perspective on the destructive effects of such a habit, so a turning to God enables us to appreciate our new calling as well as our past sin. The two are always in direct proportion. The more we appreciate our spiritual life, the more horror we feel toward sin. The less horror we feel at sin, the less we appreciate our spiritual life.

Gospel Reading

This parable, unique to Luke, underscores the need for perspective. Jesus does not excoriate wealth here. He does speak of the distraction which a desire for its accumulation can impose on other areas of our life. In the final analysis, the ultimate trigger of perspective is death. When we face the possibility of death, our values and our life style find themselves placed in a new light. We begin to see fresh significance in small things and less importance in the commercial values which our culture promotes. As one United States Senator phrased it, "I never heard of anyone on his deathbed say that he wished he had spent more time with his work."

Point

Our priorities depend on whether we live on the surface or in the deeper levels of life.

TUESDAY — Twenty-Ninth Week of the Year
Ep 2:12-22   *Lk 12:35-38*

First Reading

The Ephesians were Gentiles converted to Christianity. In Jewish eyes, they were still pagans. To capture the force of this letter, we might recall the hostility that crackled between Jewish people and everybody else in those days. The mutual antagonism had political, historical and economic roots. It also had its religious reasons. The Jewish people were chosen; everybody else was not. Within this cultural setting, Paul makes the startling assertion that in Jesus Christ, Gentiles are no longer strangers and foreigners to the promise and covenant. Every bit of the Jewish heritage that was distinctive—covenant, prophets and promised glory—now belonged to Gentiles as well. This is the backdrop for the force of Paul's images of the "new man," "the body of Christ," "citizenship in God's kingdom," "human temple," "the new family and household of God." If Jews and non-Jews are now so united, how much more should unity exist among Christians who have been baptized from birth. Our goal is less to unite people in Christ than to help people realize that they are already united as brothers and sisters in the Lord.

Gospel Reading

The parable calls for vigilance toward the Master's return. Its most direct reference is to the Lord's second coming. But there is another kind of vigilance when we await not His coming at the end of history but His coming into our lives with power. There are special times and occasions especially favorable to reconciliation and forgiveness. If we miss those special moments, they can be lost for a very long time. Historians speak of the Council of Florence centuries ago as an opportune moment for the reunion of the Western and Eastern Churches. Special historical moments occurred that favored the reunion of the Catholic and Protestant Churches. In our own lives, times come when forgiveness and reunion are especially possible. If we remain stuck in frozen positions, the moment passes and we remain divided. To retrieve past opportunities is impossible. We must be vigilant for those times when the Lord comes to us with special power and a healing word.

Point

Our love for Jesus and His Church can be expressed in many ways—especially in the sacrifices we make to preserve our unity. Such sacrifices can be as heroic as any martyrdom.

WEDNESDAY — Twenty-Ninth Week of the Year
Ep 3:2-12   *Lk 12:39-48*

First Reading

The "plan" or "design" to which Ephesians refers means that the preaching of the Gospel to the Gentiles was not an historical accident. We can, therefore, discern a pattern in exile, exodus, prophets, kingship and the entire story of Israel and Judah. Throughout this time, God was preparing a people able to say freely, "Jesus is Lord!" We can see a similar pattern in our lives. The good news of the Gospel is that God's love for us is a gift. It is not something that we can earn or buy. That was Paul's liberating and energizing insight born from his Damascus experience. The salvation he experienced in Jesus was gift, grace, free, unearned. Therefore, all grace is gift. Paul is saying that we cannot act in a certain way to earn God's love. No matter what we do, God loves us. Our effort is to be worthy of that love. He is saying that we are changed, deep down. "Act like it!" We should let the Holy Spirit we have received express Himself. When God looks within us, He sees the embryo of what we can be in Christ.

Gospel Reading

To whomever much is given, much will be required. Each of us has a titanic capacity to love, to forgive, to generate life and to show forth Christ to others. Circumstances, events and sin can cripple that capacity. Still, it is not necessary to draw the Spirit down into our life. That has already been done in baptism. Our obligation as Christians is to do all we can to let that Spirit be released from within us. To that end, we have the duty to use all available resources to enable us to develop a healthy, functioning spiritual life.

Point

To leave the uncreated energies of God within us untapped is the classic meaning of sin. To experience them is salvation.

THURSDAY — Twenty-Ninth Week of the Year
Ep 3:14-21   Lk 12:49-53

First Reading

This is a magnificent passage from the letter to the Ephesians. Paul is referring to our personal experience of Jesus Christ. This is as critical for us as it was for Paul. When we put it into words, we have the beginning of doctrine. When we put it into symbol, we have the beginning of liturgy. When we put it into action, we have the beginning of apostolate. When we put it into structures, we have the beginnings of a Christian community. When we put it into buildings, we have the beginnings of cathedrals. Jesus Christ and our experience of His love are the molten core—the magma—of the Church. Remove our personal experience of the Lord and each of these things can become an idol. Doctrine becomes ideology; liturgy becomes ceremony; apostolate becomes empire-building; and a parish becomes an administrative unit.

Gospel Reading

Today's Gospel reading reminds us not only that the experience of Jesus is central but that it is also decisive. Jesus can become vivid to us in many ways. Religious experience can take many forms. How authentic and real that experience is can be gauged from its effect in our lives: how we handle property and how we deal with others. This impact on life style is what authenticates any religious experience. The Lord's emphasis is not on generational division as much as it is on wholehearted commitment. He rejects a privatization of our faith experience. Our discipleship must be thorough, public and practical.

Point

Our personal encounter with the Lord is the fuel of our spiritual and secular life.

FRIDAY — Twenty-Ninth Week of the Year
Ep 4:1-6   *Lk 12:54-59*

First Reading

This reading leads to the second part of the letter to the Ephesians. Although it is denominated as "to the Ephesians," it probably was a circular letter passed around to several communities. Here, Paul starts to spell out the implications of all that he has said about the Church. We have had a cosmic vision of the Church's role as an agent of universal reconciliation. It is the nucleus of the world-wide restoration. When we translate this sublime vision to the local level, we must take care. It is easy to be enamored by visions of world-wide Catholicism and to forget that the dynamics of salvation are local. Our parish is the specific place where people respond to the Word of God, where the ministry of Jesus continues to take concrete shape, where people have access to the tradition. If the Pope writes an encyclical to all the world and it is neither read nor applied on the local level, for these people it is as though it had never been written. It is on the local level that the Spirit moves and where Christian love is given texture for all to feel. The people around us are the People of God to whom we are connected. They are the Body of Christ for us. The problems and limitations of our parish form the context that colors our spirituality.

Gospel Reading

We are told to watch for the signs of the times. The coming of judgment is like the coming of a weather change. We can tell when it is near. We should watch for signs of disintegration, of fissures and cracks in our personal and parish relationships. We should mend them early before they split wide open. We should try to settle such situations while we can lest they develop their own uncontrollable momentum toward collapse. The letter to the Ephesians reminds us that our failures and successes in personal and parish affairs are not an incidental sideshow. They all have a place in retarding or advancing the great design of God toward reconciling everything in Christ.

Point

Cosmic processes take place on the local level.

SATURDAY — Twenty-Ninth Week of the Year
Ep 4:7-16   *Lk 13:1-9*

First Reading

Today's first reading centers on the reality of the Incarnation. Jesus took on human nature so that He could render it malleable to the infusion of His Spirit. Paul states this tightly as Christ's "descending" in order to "ascend." That journey of the Lord entailed the sending of the Spirit to the Church so that the community He founded is now the Body of Christ in our world. He has endowed the Church with all of His gifts. All of Jesus' ministerial functions have not been given to every Christian. There is a complex and harmonious interaction among all of us which, when working together, continues Jesus' ministry in a manner more expansive and multifaceted than was ever humanly possible in Galilee. The effective functioning of a parish requires the fundamental fidelity of each of us to our baptismal commitment to Christ. This means loyalty to parish, to baptismal power and to mission. To omit any of these three hinders full development to maturity of the ecclesial Body of Christ. Without parish, we become factionalized; without mission, we become a holding action; without baptismal commitment, we forget our place in the larger design.

Gospel Reading

The success or failure of the Church or parish must be seen in the context of God's overall design. Short-run failures are not inconsistent with long-term success. The presence of sin in the Church is not inconsistent with its ecclesial holiness. The fact of decline in one part of the world does not preclude world-wide growth. Jesus reminds us not to find too facile an equivalence between the empirical and the spiritual. Physical death does not mean spiritual death. We cannot conclude that those who die tragically are evil to a degree greater than others. The Lord expands the focus to remind us that the presence or absence of fruit on a tree does not demand its immediate extinction. There is always another opportunity when the winter passes. Final judgment comes only at the very end. That is true for ourselves as well as for the Church.

Point

There are many ways to measure the success of the Gospel. Cost-benefit analysis is not one of them.

MONDAY — Thirtieth Week of the Year
Ep 4:32-5:8   *Lk 13:10-17*

First Reading

Paul's brief description of the rules of Christian living might evoke an "easier said than done" response because his section on becoming a "new person" in Christ has been omitted from the readings. That discussion is vital to understand his argument in today's reading. The Holy Spirit is present in us as a real power to do good and to live a Christian life. Baptism and confirmation direct us toward a complete and dynamic Christian life. Our difficulty lies in removing the blockages that prohibit that Spirit from pouring out of us. When there is a breakdown in our spiritual life, we then need rules. Married couples deeply in love need no outside help in communicating. When that love becomes worn and a bit dim, then they must turn to rules and books on techniques of communication. The same is true of faith. When we let the light of the Lord shine out of us, we are pulled into the dynamic flow of God's life. When there are obstructions, then we must have recourse to rules and external sources of guidance to help us through the valley.

Gospel Reading

We see the opposite side of the need for rules as an antidote for a wounded spirituality. Jesus healed on the Sabbath not because He did not respect the Sabbath but because He placed the rules into perspective. The Holy Spirit enables us to interpret and apply rules that without such wisdom can easily become the opposite of what was originally intended. Rules are not ends in themselves but tools of maturity. The uses of our communion fasting rules are examples. A rigid, precise application of the rules (58 minute fast before communion) can contravene their original purpose which is respect for the Eucharist.

Point

Rules are tools to help us grow. Their purpose is to bring us to a point where they are unnecessary.

TUESDAY — Thirtieth Week of the Year
Ep 5:21-33   *Lk 13:18-21*

First Reading

We often find ourselves in situations where we have enor-

mous power over other people. It can happen when we meet
someone especially vulnerable and we recognize that with a
few words we can deeply hurt or heal them. Paul explores the
meaning of the words "Be imitators of God" in three standard
human institutions: marriage, family and slavery. He takes
these institutions as he finds them and shows how Christians
can transform them from within.

In the case of marriage, a situation in those days of complete male dominance, he states, "Husbands, love your wives
as Christ loves the Church." Just as the Lord Jesus and the
Church are bonded, so husbands and wives should be bound
together physically, psychologically and spiritually. It would
seriously miss Paul's point to see his words as endorsing a
particular cultural arrangement. He is showing the profound
effect Christian love can have on institutions, however one-
sided they might be.

Gospel Reading

The kingdom starts small like a bit of yeast in a huge mass
of dough. Slowly, the entire thing grows. We can appreciate the
power of the Resurrection from its effects on people over the
years. In an imperfect society, we cannot simply build a Christian society from scratch. That is a psychological and philo-
sophical impossibility. Our role as Christians is to take our
society as it is and to begin to transform it from within. The easy
excuse would be to point to the mammoth size of such a task. It
is far easier to go with the flow of things as they are. "When in
Rome. . ." No single one of us can change the ethics of the
corporate world overnight. But the point which Ephesians
seeks to make is that we can slowly change our part of the
world. There is a ripple effect in the good we do. We can create
our own little apostolate which the Lord will use to affect the
whole.

Point

No institution, social arrangement or economic system is alien to Christ. He is Lord of all and can transform all from within through us.

WEDNESDAY — Thirtieth Week of the Year
Ep 6:1-9   *Lk 13:22-30*

First Reading

Paul continues to describe three special, highly-charged social relationships through which we can have powerful effects on others. He takes these institutions as he finds them and describes a Christian way of transforming them. He instructs children to obey their parents as parents try to raise them as would the Lord. Slaves should obey their masters as if they were serving Christ while Christian masters should treat their slaves as would the Lord Jesus. The challenge Paul hurls at us is that no situation is so inherently evil that we cannot find a way of reflecting Christ within it. How we manage to do that will require thoughtful prayer and intelligent consideration. There is no situation that is unredeemable. In fact, we are called to transform our situations and our lives. We are called to focus on our responsibilities and duties "in the Lord" rather than insist on our rights. A Christian atmosphere at home, work or rectory does not drop out of heaven. It is the result of prayer, thought and work.

Gospel Reading

Jesus speaks about the narrow door. There will come a time when the master shuts the door and no one will be able to enter. The immediate reference here is to the judgment and to those who have refused to enter. To all of us, it refers to our death as the time when further opportunities for us to grow in the Lord will cease. It can also refer to our opportunities in this life that we have lost. We can all recall those times in school, work or a particular relationship when someone either died or moved away with whom we were unreconciled. If we have had such an experience, we know what it is like to fail to redeem the time. Time moves on and we cannot freeze all our important opportunities in a state of cryonic suspension until we decide to address them as the Lord's disciples. Grace-filled opportunity is lost by inaction and the passage of time.

Point

Our eternity will be filled with the knowledge of opportunities lost or fulfilled.

THURSDAY — Thirtieth Week of the Year
Ep 6:10-20 *Lk 13:31-35*

First Reading

Paul uses a military metaphor to describe the Christian life. His larger point, apart from his arresting analogies, is that the Christian life is more than persuasion and good example. In fact, we are fighting the power of evil that incarnates itself in our lives in various ways. Evil can take form in ideologies, political forces, economic arrangements and social systems. In all of this, we should remember that a power greater than the sum total of our opponents is present. Just as the Christian community is not simply the sum of its members but is actuated by the Spirit of the Lord Jesus, so the forces of those who seek to diminish human dignity and crush the Spirit-inspired initiative we have are more than the sum of the opponents we can see.

They, too, are actuated by an ancient spirit—Satan, who confronted Jesus in the desert and throughout His ministry. The temptations to the Christian community are the same as those faced by the Lord in the desert. Paul reminds us that we are doing combat with a great deal more than human ignorance, human passivity and human depravity.

Gospel Reading

The Lord refers to the power of evil that can reside in political as well as religious structures. In Luke's Gospel, Jerusalem is more than a city. It is a symbol of everything that was wrong with Judaism at the time of Jesus. Jesus sets His face firmly to confront Jerusalem. We do the same in our Christian life. We confront the powers of evil in many ways. We do not do battle necessarily with bayonets, tanks and guns. Our battle is through compassion, kindness, love, prayer, service, healing, helping, comforting, assisting. We do not confront evil with more evil (under a religious banner). We confront evil with good as did Jesus. We share in the same victory He had. Otherwise, we become like our enemies.

Point

In the secular world, battles brutalize victor and victim. In the spiritual realm, battle can elevate both.

FRIDAY — Thirtieth Week of the Year
Ph 1:1-11   *Lk 14:1-6*

First Reading

The letter to the Philippians is one of Paul's last letters, written to the first Church he founded in Europe. It was written while he was in prison. Its tone is one of retrospective on his apostleship. The community at Philippi was deepest in his affection and strongest in loyalty to him. They "helped promote the Gospel from the very first day." We can note two things about today's first reading. When Paul speaks about the "Gospel" he preaches, he is referring not to a book but to a tradition about Jesus. It refers to Paul's preaching, style of life and a certain kind of communal life he endorsed. In short, the "Gospel" is a way of life. Secondly, Paul prays that the Philippians may learn to value the things that really matter. The Greek word he uses is close to our English word "aesthetic"— almost like an intuition or "sixth sense" about things pertaining to the faith. There is a natural sense of right and wrong which is enhanced by the Gospel to give us a spiritual savvy. In any field or profession, there is a sixth sense of what is or is not appropriate. In the same way, in our Christian lives we develop the ability to discern what is genuine from what is simply "hype," what is really of the Holy Spirit and what is not.

Gospel Reading

There is a difference between Jesus' concept of religion and that of his contemporaries. They had great reverence for the Law in all of its parts. It was the best way of giving honor to God. It was an absolute test of fidelity and was given expression in the Sabbath rest. Jesus did not diminish Jewish respect for the Sabbath but saw meeting human need as a deeper way of fulfilling that Law's intent. Love of others is a way of showing love for God. The Christian does not need to choose between caring for cathedrals and caring for the poor. Both can be held together. Love of God and of people are not mutually exclusive. In fact, they are intrinsically connected.

Point

The Christian instinct takes Creation and Incarnation as two phases of one design. We need not divide our love.

SATURDAY — Thirtieth Week of the Year
Ph 1:18-26   *Lk 14:1, 7-11*

First Reading

The preaching of the Gospel rather than self-promotion is Paul's primary concern in today's first reading. If he lives or dies, Christ will still be exalted through him. Paul puts his finger on the only priority that can enable a Christian to keep spiritual sanity. It is very easy to identify our success as Christians with the success of the preaching of the Gospel. Subtle self-promotion can do strange things to a Christian's mind. It can turn another individual's rejection of the Gospel into a personal rejection of us or vice versa. It can transmute personal differences into issues of heresy. We are vital instruments of the Lord in our time and place. But the enterprise of the Gospel is wider than ourselves. If we keep our attention on Christ's promise of the Gospel's ultimate triumph, we can rest with the knowledge that our failures and successes have had some part in bringing about that result. This gives a powerful rationale to every Christian life. However the results appear to us, the Lord has used us in His own way to further the kingdom. We are part of a larger spiritual whole.

Gospel Reading

Those who spend time exalting themselves and their place in the Church will be humbled. Two dangers face us: underestimating the role we play in the Christian drama, and overestimating our importance in salvation history. If no Christian life is pointless, neither is it indispensable. While we live, we are integral components of the Church militant. But we remain servants. We are not sole proprietors of the Risen Spirit of Christ.

Point

We are all absolutely important but not indispensable parts of God's plan.

MONDAY — Thirty-First Week of the Year
Ph 2:1-4   *Lk 14:12-14*

First Reading

Much as a father is comforted by harmony among his children, Paul asks the Philippians to encourage him by striving for greater unity and harmony among themselves. It seems that no major quarrel had split the Philippian community. As with all human groupings, petty jealousies existed which, left unchecked, could lead to major disruptions. Paul suggests that while basic unity existed among them, they should make the effort to overcome minor rifts. If those tiny cracks should widen, they would become less manageable and threaten the unity in spirit and of ideals that existed in the Philippian community. Paul's concrete suggestion is that each seek the well-being of the other over his or her individual interest. When self-interest is placed in the service of all, community good becomes the major priority of all and narcissistic self-absorption has no chance to gain a foothold. The issue is sharpened for us when we examine whether we see ourselves primarily as members of a faith community or as individual Christians who happen to be attached to a parish without any deep personal involvement therein. If it is the latter case, we can easily become self-preoccupied.

Gospel Reading

Jesus uses the example of inviting the needy to dinner to ensure that our concern for others is authentic. The motions of

Christian charity can mask aspirations very much at variance with the Christian ideal. The motives of notoriety, public holiness, the accumulation of indebtedness from others and the flight from the ordinary and anonymous can all support our work for those in need. It is only when there is no chance for personal and social remuneration that we can be certain that we are acting out of sincere love and not from self-interest that masquerades as Christian love.

Point

Concern for others can be motivated by self-enhancement or self-sacrifice.

TUESDAY — Thirty-First Week of the Year
Ph 2:5-11   *Lk 14:15-24*

First Reading

Self-righteousness or a sense of spiritual superiority is a temptation of every age. In a famous section of the letter to the Philippians, Paul instructs them that their attitude must be like that of Jesus who took the form of a slave in complete obedience to the Father. Because of His total obedience, He was made Lord of all. We should notice that Paul does not deny the saving power of Christ's passion and death. He is probing more deeply into this gesture to locate the passion's saving power in Christ's obedience to the Father even to the point of death. That obedience gave His death saving force. The same is true for all of Christ's disciples. It is not the difficult circumstances of our life or our pain that carry spiritual power. It is our obedience and faithful endurance and spiritual transformation of that pain into prayer that charges it with saving power for ourselves and for others. Millions of people suffer each day across our planet. Suffering offered faithfully to the Father in Christ (knowingly or not) has redeeming power and can shift spiritual energy to others.

Gospel Reading

Self-righteousness prevented the Jewish leaders from accepting Jesus' offer of entry into the kingdom experience of God. They were convinced that they had a lock on God. The Lord tells a parable addressed to this very attitude. The invitees refused to come for a variety of lame excuses. The invitation did not seem important to them. The host of this pro-Gentile parable turned to the outcasts who recognized their hunger and need. The Gospel follows a similar history. The saving word of Jesus can be delayed or discarded by those who feel spiritually satisfied. They have nothing further to learn from the familiar Gospel words. Their spiritual growth has ceased and decline has set in without their being aware of it. It is only those who recognize their shortcomings, their pockets of sin and failure in their lives and their further need of the Lord whom the Gospel invitation reaches and touches. Both groups hear the same words, but one is willing to follow the Lord beyond the ordinary.

Point

Inward attitudes give spiritual shape to our outward behavior.

WEDNESDAY — Thirty-First Week of the Year
Ph 2:12-18   *Lk 14:25-33*

First Reading

Paul tells the Philippians to work to achieve their salvation. He is not asking that they find some way to save themselves but that they try to actualize and bring to life the Spirit they have received in baptism. He advises them to live a straightforward life in a wicked world. They are not to isolate themselves from the rest of the world but to make a creative effort to redeem their culture. It is difficult but important that someone maintain integrity in what has been called a "rip-off" society. A great deal of intelligent effort is demanded, especially today, to find ways of being a practical Christian who can effectively witness to the Gospel message and the presence of the Lord.

Gospel Reading

Against the background of yesterday's parable of the great dinner and the invitation of straggling hitch-hikers into the hall, Jesus makes a further point. Discipleship should not be impulsive. It requires careful and conscious acceptance. This is the message of the parables of the farmer and the warrior king. What draws these readings together is the fact that spiritual life and discipleship require method. Effective following of the Lord demands planning to integrate our faith into the various sectors of our life. Unless we do, such integration will be done haphazardly, in an illusory fashion. It will come to seem too formidable and then be discarded as impractical. Likewise, our spiritual life is not the result of accident or chance. It also requires method and planning. We must have an accurate knowledge of ourselves and know the lessons that can be distilled from the history of spirituality. Otherwise, we might lock ourselves into an approach to spiritual growth that is wrong or psychologically inappropriate for our individual selves. The Lord cautions us, therefore, to be wise in the ways of the soul as we are in the ways of the world.

Point

Growth in the spiritual life, as in the stock market, requires strategy.

THURSDAY — Thirty-First Week of the Year
Ph 3:3-8   *Lk 15:1-10*

First Reading

Paul looks back over his life as a highly orthodox Jew. In terms of religious observance, he had a perfect score. He was everything that an ideal Pharisaic Jew was supposed to be. Now, in the light of his Damascus road experience, he looks back and affirms that compared with the knowledge of Jesus Christ, all of his past was like a gigantic loss. What he had thought were spiritual "assets" were, in fact, liabilities. They were a misplaced faith that prevented him from realizing his need and the capacity of the Risen Lord to fill that need. Paul's experience illustrates the fact that the seed of repentance and renewing change is present in every person. We all have within us the power to turn and return. The capacity for conversion and repentance lies within us like a powerful spotlight waiting to be set off to expose the areas of darkness and light within our lives.

Gospel Reading

Jesus delivers two brief parables of the lost sheep and the lost coin to show the Father's joy in a single sinner's repentance. People who repent, turn and convert are not second-class citizens brought back home to a recriminatory chorus of "I told you so." That is not the Christian style of reconciliation. Instead, they are welcomed back and placed at the head of the table. As exemplified in Paul's life, the search and reach of the Lord to those who have fallen or who are on the outside is wide indeed. He gives hundreds of opportunities to every individual to trigger conversion. Many refuse to respond. We all have friends and relatives who seem indifferent to the faith. Planted within that individual is the seed of change and the power of heroic faith waiting to be released. Those who do respond to the Lord's call are the stuff of great conversion stories. Precisely because the capacity for faith is within them, however dormant, we should not abandon any person but recall them in our prayers. We never know what prayer or word of ours will unlock the power within them.

Point

We never know what event or word will release the great spiritual potential locked within every individual.

FRIDAY — Thirty-First Week of the Year
Ph 3:17-4:1   *Lk 16:1-8*

First Reading

In today's first reading, Paul suggests that the Philippians imitate him or, by extension, the saints. Frequently, we reduce the spiritual life to a series of abstract axioms and never advert to the shape it takes in concrete lives. This is the value of the lives of holy people over time. When we read the stories of Paul, Francis, Dominic, Ignatius, Maximilian Kolbe and many others, we see the permutations and combinations that the single Gospel message takes in different cultural climates with different requirements. The spiritual life is not invariant under cultural transformation. Its twists and turns differ with different contexts. Very often, we fail to manage our spiritual growth. We leave it dormant until a crisis arises. We then try to react in a spiritual way only to discover that we have not developed the spiritual equipment to deal with the problems that confront us. The lives of the saints provide marvelous examples of the adaptability and creativity of God's people in answering the Lord's call throughout a bewildering variety of circumstances.

Gospel Reading

An agent is caught cheating and then uses the opportunity he has to pad his own future. We expect Jesus to condemn the man. Instead, He holds him up as an example of resourceful-ness. This parable has the same effect today that it had when the Lord first told it. It was meant to shock. The Lord's lesson is as accurate as it is dramatic. In our society, people are very concerned about health and appearance and become expert in the literature of nutrition, coping and health. Many become expert in the techniques of tax, estate and financial planning. Yet, the entire area of the spiritual life is generally neglected. Every person has a spiritual life with its own rhythms and dynamics. A whole body of literature exists which describes the geography of this region of the soul. There are subtleties to the Spirit's work within us as well as to our pitfalls. Familiarity with these facts of the spiritual life is what the Lord encourages.

Point

As our knowledge of all areas of human life expands, many of us remain children in our understanding of the spiritual life.

SATURDAY — Thirty-First Week of the Year
Ph 4:10-19   Lk 16:9-15

First Reading

Paul concludes his letter to the Philippians with a word of gratitude for their support and encouragement during the dif-ficult time of his ministry. It is a touching sentiment of an apostle at the end of his work. Paul describes how he has learned to cope in the Lord with success and failure. We often forget that Paul probably thought at the outset that the Gospel would spread like wildfire throughout the world. He quickly discovered that Church politics, the popular apathy of people without the religious experience he had, and old enemies would hamper both his ministry and the movement of the Gospel. Throughout his letters, we can trace the various successes and failures of his efforts, and how he commended both to the Lord. The same is the case with ourselves. In a flush of enthusiasm, we expect spiritual growth and fruitfulness to accompany all our efforts. As time passes, we learn there are spiritual alleys, dark nights, and personal collisions along the way. Yet, if we keep our trust in the Lord and His Spirit within us, we learn to commend our moments of darkness and of light to Him.

Gospel Reading

Jesus encourages us to use our talents, abilities and resources to maintain harmony with those around us. When difficulties come, we will have the internal strength and spiritual network to sustain us. How we deal with material goods is more susceptible to control than how we deal with motives, feelings, temptations and inspirations that cross our minds and hearts every day. Often, we do not have the expertise to deal with these more intimate and more powerful forces. We must choose a principle of orientation. That principle will either be the Lord or material success. We cannot keep two lords in our life in perfect balance. One will dominate. Dealing with this prioritizing is a learned ability. It is not jammed into us at our baptism. Over a lifetime, like Paul, we learn to control not events but our responses to them.

Point

To control our own selves requires more effort and grace than to control acres of real estate.

MONDAY — Thirty-Second Week of the Year
Tt 1:1-9   *Lk 17:1-6*

First Reading

The letter to Titus, together with two letters to Timothy, make up the "pastoral" letters of Paul. They provide an invaluable insight into the structure and personnel of the first Christian communities. In this reading, Paul speaks of "presbyters" who may or may not be exactly equivalent to our modern bishops. What is striking in Paul's letter is his expectations of these presbyters. He does not look for brilliance or mystical experiences but common sense and balance. The men who are to lead Christian communities should be people of personal and theological moderation. They are to guard the faith which in this letter is identical with doctrine. We can see, at this point, a gradual emergence of the Church as a Catholicism with an organized structure and a fairly coherent, if inchoate, set of doctrines. These provide the outward organizational principles of the emerging and growing Catholic community.

Gospel Reading

Jesus speaks about faith in a sense different from that of doctrine. He refers to faith as an act of personal trust. This has sometimes been called the "experience of God." The Lord describes the power of such faith. It can transform our perception of the world. We see the same items as before but in a new way—as the work of God filled with His guiding Presence. Beneath the ordinary tensions of daily living, we can discern a conflict between good and evil. This faith also has power to change our world. Faith has real, live effects. Prayer works. How, when, why it works remains unknown to us. But the cumulative evidence of the effect of prayer is so overwhelming that it cannot be attributed to mere coincidence or auto-suggestion.

The "faith" and faith go together. Of the two, inner faith is more fundamental because it is that to which doctrine gives expression. Your faith and my faith are not isolated or independent of each other. They are linked together and slowly cohere into tradition. Tradition is our faith experience as a Church. It is a powerful, rich repository of the experience of God.

Point

Tradition and doctrine give us the tools to focus, sharpen and deepen our personal experience of the Lord.

TUESDAY — Thirty-Second Week of the Year
Tt 2:1-8, 11-14   *Lk 17:7-10*

First Reading

The pastoral epistles are addressed in good part to clergy of all eras. Paul instructs the young Titus about the ministry he must exercise to all segments of the community. A presbyter or bishop has an obligation to speak the Lord's word to young and old, to wealthy and poor. There is no segment of the Christian community that is beyond reproach or guidance. There is no economic or social level of the Christian community that is beyond criticism or encouragement. If a Church leader is excessively deferential to a particular portion of the community, he is doing those very people and the Church at large a great disfavor. The unadulterated Gospel has been entrusted, as Paul repeatedly tells us, not to angels but to people. The Gospel is to be preached through the presbyters commissioned as its agents. This is the reason for Paul's strong admonitions to speak words of truth and correction to everybody. Furthermore, as we move beyond superficial distinctions among Christians, we come to realize that spiritual needs and problems are the same whether a Christian lives in Palm Springs or Watts.

Gospel Reading

Our service to the Gospel is not an extraordinary achievement for which we should expect praise. This is the thrust of the Lord's words in today's Gospel passage. When we have exhausted ourselves in the service of the Word and done our best, we should realize that that is exactly what Jesus expects us to do. He has, after all, given us the stamina and ability to so fruitfully work for the Gospel. In other words, there is no standard level of achievement in Gospel living beyond which we earn extra points. We are called to do our best and our most for the Lord.

Point

Our service of the Gospel is to all the people all the time.

WEDNESDAY — Thirty-Second Week of the Year
Tt 3:1-7   *Lk 17:11-19*

First Reading

Paul tells Titus that spiritual renewal affects social and political harmony. Some Marxists assert that if people are broken within, the cause lies in the corruption of the system in which they live. Change the system and you will change the people. It is a recommendation for change from the outside in. Mainline Christian thinkers have asserted that the process is reversed. We must first seek to change people from within in order to transform society. Change works from the inside out. If thieves are placed in charge of a perfect social structure, they will corrupt the system. Personal transformation is prior to societal change. The condition of society mirrors what is in people's hearts. The condition of a parish or family reflects what is going on in the souls of its members.

Gospel Reading

Ten lepers were cured and only one, a Samaritan, returned to give thanks. To this one individual, Jesus says that his faith has been his salvation. Ten were healed physically but only one was made spiritually whole. For that single Samaritan, his physical cure was an occasion for personal transformation. He was healed within. We have a contrast between physical healing and inner healing. Perhaps one of the points Luke is making is that inner healing is the more important. When our faith in Christ is deep, secure and rooted, if our center holds firm, then the other parts of our lives in parish, family and society begin to hang together.

Point

The coherence of a community reflects peace at its center.

THURSDAY — Thirty-Second Week of the Year
Phm 7-20   *Lk 17:20-25*

First Reading

Philemon was a wealthy Christian whose slave escaped after being attracted by the bright lights of Rome. This runaway slave ran into Paul who converted him ("whose father I am") and Paul now sends him back to the owner no longer as a slave but as a baptized brother in the Lord. Paul is requesting Philemon to let faith in the Lord transform this otherwise brutal relationship of master and slave. Through the faith they share, this demeaning arrangement can become redemptive for both of them. No society is perfect and completely reflective of the dominion of God. That is a dimension and stage to which we are called to bring it. Nevertheless, the assertion implicit in Paul's note is that everything is open to the healing power of the Lord.

Gospel Reading

Jesus does not identify the kingdom with any regime, culture or economic system. Everything falls short of the full, public mastery by God. The kingdom is a product of God's own making. Yet, the kingdom is not a completely remote event. The Lord tells us repeatedly that it has an anticipatory existence within the human heart. The kingdom is within you, in your midst, within your grasp. Its decisive public and enduring appearance awaits God's own time. But that does not indicate that it is totally absent from our scene. What is important is that we not too quickly identify the reign of God with any political or economic system. Too facile an equivalence will lead to disappointment as well as to the investment of human achievements with a sanction and authority they do not deserve.

Point

The kingdom of God reminds us that every earthly structure, secular or sacred, is subject to a higher Judgment.

FRIDAY — Thirty-Second Week of the Year
2 Jn 4-9   Lk 17:26-37

First Reading

The second letter of John, maybe a "memo" attached to the first letter, states that many deceitful men have departed from the community who do not acknowledge Jesus as having come in the flesh. There is a cluster of doctrines known collectively as Docetism which stem from a severe separation of matter and spirit such that the body and flesh are seen to be evil. Therefore, an all-good God cannot have contact with it. As a result, the Lord Jesus merely pretended or appeared to be human. The letter condemns such a "costume Christology" as a product of the anti-Christ forces. The reaction is so violent because Docetism touched the very jugular of Catholicism.

Because the Spirit of God infused matter in the Incarnation, our theology is sacramental. The Spirit can infuse bread, wine and sacramental gestures. If Jesus was pretending in Galilee, He is pretending in the sacraments. Their effect is then only psychological and not ontological. A question fundamental to Catholicism is whether in the liturgy and in the Church we are making real contact with the Lord or not. This was the issue that so exercised the Johannine community.

Gospel Reading

There are several reasons for the Lord's caution about excessive speculation about the last days. If the Second Coming were on a set date, people would be indifferent until that date. Secondly, if the judgment will set people apart, it is clear that until that moment we cannot easily segregate the saved and the unsaved. Our judgments must always remain provisional. Thirdly, Jesus broadens the message of the judgment to any moment of decision. Important decisions throughout our lives have far reaching and perhaps eternal consequences. People can set their own final judgment when they shut the Lord out of their lives forever. As far as they are concerned, for them that is a final judgment.

Point

Judgment and salvation, sin and grace are not simply

psychological events. They are real ingredients in our life here. That is the meaning and power of the Incarnation.

SATURDAY — Thirty-Second Week of the Year
3 Jn 5-8   *Lk 18:1-8*

First Reading

This third letter, actually a "note," of John concerns fellow-Christians who are strangers to our town. We can apply its message both to missionaries and Christians in other parts of the world. It would be a scandal if parts of a parish starved while other members of the same parish dined regularly at expensive restaurants. Yet, that is a daily fact of life in the world-wide Church. Economically, we have a bunching of resources—personnel and money—in certain dioceses while other areas of the Church both in this country and in the world are in tragically dire need. John's admonition to all of us is to examine our responsibilities to our brothers and sisters in the Lord who are in serious need. To the extent that we have resources to assist them, to that extent we have a duty before Christ to do so.

Gospel Reading

Jesus speaks about the inevitability of God's judgment. It is a judgment that can take many forms. It can even be a judgment against the Church. If we are selfish with our resources, there will come a time when our need will not be met by others. Once upon a time, the Church in North Africa was wealthy and vibrant. When hard times fell, there was no one to assist it. Today, that segment of the Church is virtually extinct. The cross of Christ falls upon all sections of the Church, but in various ways. If hunger plagues the Church in Africa, affluence brings its own temptations to the Church in some parts of North

America. Any of these crosses seriously tempt a person's faith. Will any faith be left when the Lord returns? But with our ability to help one another, much as a body can transfer healing resources to limbs in need, the faith can not only survive but thrive in power.

Point

The community Jesus founded is interdependent on the local and international levels. However widely distributed, it remains the single community of Jesus.

MONDAY — Thirty-Third Week of the Year
Rv 1:1-4; 2:1-5   *Lk 18:35-43*

First Reading

The Book of Revelation is at once the most obscure and the most fascinating of the New Testament writings. It is filled with strange symbols some of which we can decipher and others whose significance is forever lost to us. It was written for first century Christians with a meaning for every generation. This explains its widespread use, perennial attraction and the popularity of its symbols of the Antichrist and Armageddon. In reading this book, we should not become lost in the individual symbols but keep our eye on its central theme. The event that occasioned the book was the conflict between the Roman Empire and the early Christians. The writer saw universal implications in these events. He saw the eternal conflict between Satan and God; the spirit of evil and the Spirit of Christ. The persecution which these Christians were enduring was one phase of a much larger drama. Today's first reading begins the letters to the seven churches. These were individual Christian communities each of which had difficulties and fell prey to temptations which are recurrent in the Church. The Church at Ephesus had done heroic work defending the faith and fighting off error. But they had forgotten why. They lost their first love for the Lord and possibly for each other. They had become more interested in the fight than in what they had been fighting for.

Gospel Reading

The restoration of a man's sight stands for the gift of spiritual sight that we call faith. Luke could look at physical healing to see within it a universal spiritual truth. Within the individual events of our lives are embedded universal principles, truths and axioms. We drop a book. It is an instance of the law of gravity. We need spiritual sight to see beyond the conflicts that wrack our life to the larger drama of which we are a part. Like the Church at Ephesus, we can so emphasize the institutional truths and defenses of the Church that we can forget that it is also a community. These two dimensions need each other. They are not artificially connected. We can so emphasize law, rights and structure that we fail to notice that the soul of our community is love and Spirit.

Point

Spiritual sight sees beyond our institutional conflicts to the crises of love.

TUESDAY — Thirty-Third Week of the Year
Rv 3:1-6, 14-22   *Lk 19:1-10*

First Reading

The failings of the two churches in today's readings are

opposite: activism and apathy. To the Church at Sardis, the Lord says, "I know your reputation of being alive." Perhaps they were culturally dynamic or religiously active with all sorts of committees and subcommittees. Whichever was the case, they were spiritually dead. It was an empty activism. They were spinning wheels, doing what was spiritually fashionable and simply lurching from enthusiasm to enthusiasm. It looked like a great deal was going on, but nothing was really happening. All the activity was a way of covering up and anesthetizing their spiritual bankruptcy.

The Church at Laodicea had two major industries: banking and medicine. They go together. This Church receives the most severe reprimand because it had become apathetic. It was too self-satisfied, too careful and cautious. One great enemy of Christianity is affluence. It is difficult to see shortcomings in the establishment when you are part of it. For the Laodiceans, Christianity had become another piece of cultural furniture. Their material well-being hid their spiritual poverty. Activist Sardis and apathetic Laodicea were opposite expressions of spiritual emptiness.

Gospel Reading

Zacchaeus provides a contrast with these churches. He shows great spiritual energy as he goes out of his way to see the Lord and welcome Him to his home. Zacchaeus was a professional outcast. Upon meeting Jesus, or perhaps even before that, he gave half his property to the poor and recompensed those he had defrauded several times over. In this extraordinary effort to secure justice, he shows himself to be a genuine son of Abraham. Perhaps it was his outcast status that enabled him to appreciate the importance of justice and the power of the Lord's words of forgiveness.

Point

Zacchaeus differed from the trendy Sardians and the apathetic Laodiceans in that he actively sought the Lord and sought to do right with his neighbors as well.

WEDNESDAY — Thirty-Third Week of the Year
Rv 4:1-11   *Lk 19:11-28*

First Reading

This reading begins the second part of the Book of Revelation. It is important to remember that the Book of Revelation appeals primarily to the imagination. It is not heavily conceptual as are the letters to the Romans and Galatians. It is a kind of multi-media expression of a powerful religious vision. It is the Word of God given to us not primarily through concepts but through images. In this reading, we have a vision of the glory and majesty of God as the great scenario begins: the seven seals, seven trumpets, Dragon, Lamb, seven bowls, the fall of Babylon and the Second Coming of Christ. The purpose of this writing is to enable Christians to endure great tribulations by assuring them that events are not haphazard and that their safe outcome is secured in God's hands. This scene of God in His glory is the calm before the storm.

Gospel Reading

The Gospel reading is also about preparing for the storm. The parable of the talents, into which Luke weaves a second parable, presents a test for the Church as well as for individuals. We have been given specific spiritual gifts, the Holy Spirit, our intelligence—and the issue is what we have accomplished with them. Does the Church hide its gifts, suppress its talents, remain frozen, place itself on the defensive—or does it expand and develop its grace to release its power? We can perform the same kind of self-examination in regard to our personal spiritual gifts. We can ask whether our spiritual life is any better than it was ten years ago. Have we used all the talents the Lord has given us only to improve our lives financially and socially? Have we used our gifts to come to better know the Lord? Just as the Pharisees who preserved but did not expand their heritage, so the Church and ourselves will be called to account for what we have been given.

Point

If we have been given gifts, they are for a reason.

THURSDAY — Thirty-Third Week of the Year
Rv 5:1-10   *Lk 19:41-44*

First Reading

We should not concentrate on individual details in the Book of Revelation as much as on the overall picture. The entire impression is important. Yesterday's reading portrayed God in His glory in heaven. Now, events begin to unfold. In today's reading, there is a scroll containing the meaning of history. We often ask whether there is a pattern to historical events. It is not an academic issue but a question that spontaneously arises when we are faced with tragedy or persecution as were these early Christians. We search for purpose and value. The answer is contained in the scroll which nobody is capable of opening until the Lamb, symbol of the Risen Christ, appears and takes it. Jesus Christ is the Lord of history: both universal history and our individual stories as well. He not only controls the final outcome but helps us see the value of individual events. If their meaning is not clear as crystal to us, then we can trust and hope in His love. The message of this section of Revelation is that the conclusion of human history is not up for grabs. The forces of evil will not completely exterminate the faithful although they will be present in power until the very end.

Gospel Reading

Jesus speaks about the end. There are many levels on which we can think about this subject. We can consider the end of the cosmos. We can discuss the end of our "world" in the sense of the end of an era. Such was the cultural shift that occurred after World War II as well as centuries earlier with the destruction of Jerusalem. We can also speak about the end of our lives. The Gospels and the Book of Revelation can be read and applied on each of these levels. In each instance, the struggle is not over until we are completely in the presence of Christ. That is the only point at which we will be assured of complete peace, final resolution and victory. Until then, we live by faith.

Point

The Lamb, the Risen Christ, alone knows the why and wherefore of the human story. We trust in Him.

FRIDAY — Thirty-Third Week of the Year
Rv 10:8-11   *Lk 19:45-48*

First Reading

Between yesterday's reading and today's, we skipped five chapters. Let us summarize those interim events. The Lamb was given the great scroll with seven seals containing the meaning of history. He broke the seals one by one and each time its contents were shown visually. The first four seals revealed the four horsemen: war, death, famine and defeat. The fifth seal released the cry of the martyrs of every age. The sixth seal revealed earthquakes and revolution. When the seventh seal was broken, there was silence. Then the seven angels sound their trumpets. The first six trumpets herald natural disasters. Then, before the seventh trumpet sounds, we have today's reading. John is instructed to eat the small scroll, that is, to assimilate and make its message part of him. It tasted sweet and bitter. The message of a glorious salvation also says that a struggle must come first. There will be a necessary cleansing.

Gospel Reading

A cleansing of our individual temples is also important before we can experience the power of salvation. We can apply Jesus' gesture to ourselves and to our parishes. Our relationship to the Lord is something that has to be worked out, molded and fashioned, sometimes even hammered out. A living faith, a peaceful center of stillness and power in the Lord is not an accident nor something into which we stumble. Paradoxical as it may sound, peace at our center is the product of a terrific struggle until we conquer that little portion of ourselves where we can be at peace with the Lord.

Point

Profound peace is always obtained at a price. Peace easily obtained is easily fractured. Peace obtained with great effort is only broken with great effort.

SATURDAY — Thirty-Third Week of the Year
Rv 11:4-12 *Lk 20:27-40*

First Reading

This is a difficult and highly metaphorical passage. The two witnesses are Elijah (who caused a great drought) and Moses (who turned the Nile into blood). They represent prophecy and Law. Jewish tradition believed they would return before the end to announce the Day of the Lord. John intends these figures to refer to the Church. The Church will preach the Gospel (Law and prophets fulfilled) and be persecuted until the very end. One of the central messages of the Book of Revelation is that evil will exist until the end of history. There is no theory of social perfection here. The Church, represented by these two witnesses, will be persecuted not only for its doctrine but for its message of social justice as well. There will never come a time when the Church will be totally at peace—hence, it is called the Church militant. It is, perhaps, a guarantee of the truth of the Church's mission that she is always, somewhere, persecuted. The age of martyrs will continue until the end. Then, at the Lord's public return, those slain for the Gospel will rise in glory, transformed after the pattern of the Lord.

Gospel Reading

Jesus subverts an attempt to ridicule the notion of resurrection from the dead by cautioning His questioners that life after death is not explainable in terms of life in this world. The Sadducees could not square the mandate of the Levirate marriage (Dt 25:5) with personal immortality. As in the case of Jesus' Resurrection, eternal life is both discontinuous and continuous with life here. Jesus was the same person after the Resurrection as before. The Gospels go out of their way to make that point. But the kind of life He enjoyed was transformed. That same kind of triumphant and glorious existence awaits those who have been faithful to the Gospel. It is the promise of this eternal life that has provided strength for the weary and vigor for martyrs called to witness to the Gospel.

Point

The eternal existence promised the saints can be ours today in a sacramental way. That too gives us strength for our journey.

MONDAY — Thirty-Fourth Week of the Year
Rv 14:1-3, 4-5   *Lk 21:1-4*

First Reading

To get the full impact of today's reading, we should quickly rehearse the section immediately preceding it. That section described the emergence of two beasts, whom we may call Leviathan and Behemoth. Today's reading then contrasts the people of God with those who worship the beast. The Book of Revelation is filled with elusive figures. Who is the beast? For the early Christians it was the Roman Empire. But the beast as well as the Antichrist and the infamous "666" are all open categories for us. Over the centuries, they have been filled by all kinds of characters, movements and philosophies. We bring our own conflicts into our reading of these chapters. In contrast to those who worship the beast are those who remain faithful. If the presence of evil is with us until the very end, so is the presence of faith and love. The presence of grace in our world is as widespread as that of sin but less publicized. Our difficulty is that they do not carry clear labels. They intermingle and mix.

Gospel Reading

The conflict between good and evil is graphically shown in today's Gospel reading. The pompous teachers of the Law are set off against the poor widow who drops her few coins into the collection box. She represented the best that Judaism had to offer. The presence of saving grace among the Jews is shown in the person of this poor widow. She embodied the faith of Abraham, Isaac and Jacob. She would be instrumental in fulfilling the covenant with David and the soaring visions of Isaiah and Ezekiel. She was the remnant that God promised would always be there. It is from people such as her that Jesus would fashion a new Israel.

Point

The presence of evil and grace pervade history. Their clash creates the dynamic of salvation history.

TUESDAY — Thirty-Fourth Week of the Year
Rv 14:14-19   *Lk 21:5-11*

First Reading

We have probably had our fill of the visions of the Book of Revelation. Two things need to be said about today's first reading. The first is that it is the source of many literary phrases we know: "the grim reaper," "fire and brimstone," "God's trampling out the vintage where the grapes of wrath are stored." Sickles and winepresses signify waves and waves of destruction and terror. Preoccupation with a detailed interpretation of the Book of Revelation has never been important in mainstream Catholicism. One reason for this is that many

fundamentalist preachers have identified the Catholic Church
with many of the symbols of evil from the Book of Revelation.

Gospel Reading

Some reasons for Catholic reticence about Revelation are
found in today's Gospel reading. Firstly, it is easy to ideologize
the events of the end of the world and use them for political
purposes. Secondly, it is easy to capitalize on natural fear about
the end and announce oneself as the agent of the coming Lord.
Thirdly, today's reading is an antidote to preoccupation with
the details of the Lord's coming. Many events have to occur
first. We saw a similar point made by Paul to the Thessalonians
and to the Corinthians. The Catholic Church has always placed
a greater emphasis on the moment of death as the angle from
which we should read the Book of Revelation. Death is the end
of our personal world and an event sure to come in our lifetime.
This is the moment for which we ought to properly prepare. A
cosmic end will come in God's time. But we should not expend
a great deal of energy speculating about its timetable. We
should look to the end that we will all inevitably face.

Point

*Preparation for our own death is much more redemptive
than is speculation about the end of the world.*

WEDNESDAY — Thirty-Fourth Week of the Year
Rv 15:1-4   *Lk 21:12-19*

First Reading

We are coming to a climax of God's wrath. This is one of

the songs of His coming victory. Those who had conquered the beast stood on the glassy sea and sang the hymn of triumph. Although the Book of Revelation portrays the clash between good and evil, between Christ and Antichrist in powerful symbols as a spectacular combat, we should not forget that we meet that same struggle in hundreds of ordinary ways from day to day in our dealings with others and in the choices we make. We should not let the epic version of this conflict that we have been viewing in living technicolor in the Book of Revelation distract us from the realization that we are currently involved in that battle in many unspectacular ways.

Gospel Reading

We switch from talk of the beast and of cryptic numbers to Jesus' statement that "*people* will persecute you, drag you into prisons and courts . . . you will be delivered up by your relatives." Precisely because the struggle takes place in many subtle ways, we cannot rehearse for it. Hence the Lord tells us not to plan in anticipation. We should prepare ourselves by prayer and cultivation of the gift of the Spirit. Because the challenges facing each of us differ, there is no standard operating procedure for what we are to do. No one can tell us beforehand how to act in facing down the different forms of evil we will encounter. We can only equip ourselves and develop our spiritual inner resources.

Point

If we render ourselves responsive to God's Spirit, we will do the right thing, almost instinctively.

THURSDAY — Thirty-Fourth Week of the Year
Rv 18:1-2, 21-23; 19:1-3, 9   *Lk 21:20-28*

First Reading

Both readings are heavy with metaphor. Historically, the great Babylon is probably Rome which would undergo destruction several centuries later. Babylon really represents any coalition of corrupt power—economic, political, military or religious. If history makes any testimony plain, it is as a witness to the transience of power. The accrual of military or economic might is no insurance that a nation will last forever. There is no guarantee of institutional or governmental immortality. If kingdoms and governments fall, what has endured is the kingdom of the Spirit—that community of faithful people of every age who have placed their hope in the Lord. The early and very fragile Christian community survived not only in memory and in its writings but also through our continuity with it in the celebration of the Eucharist. The immortality of which we can be certain derives from our link with the Risen Lord through faith. That alone survives.

Gospel Reading

Jesus describes the coming devastation of Jerusalem. Luke's recasting of the Lord's words may well have been influenced by his memory of the actual destruction that occurred forty years after the Ascension. In Luke's Gospel, Jerusalem is the symbol of entrenched power. The Lord's words can be applied, as can all eschatological statements, to history, to ourselves and to individual events. The message of Jesus here is that evil carries within itself its own inherently destructive tendency. At some point it explodes from within. The same is true of sin. It is less that we are punished for our sins than that we are destroyed by them.

Point

If love is constructive and enlarging, evil is destructive and demeaning.

FRIDAY — Thirty-Fourth Week of the Year
Rv 20:1-4, 11-21:2   Lk 21:29-33

First Reading

This passage about the thousand year chaining of the beast gave rise to various millenarian movements in the Protestant Church. Catholic interpreters see this period as referring to the Lord's reign in the Church for an extended period of time. The exact number of years is more a figure of speech than a prediction. The new heaven and new earth are centered around a new Jerusalem. The final result of world history and of all the cleansing that took place at exhausting length throughout Revelation is a new community fashioned by God. The goal of God's plan is more than individual salvation. It is a renewed and transformed community. This community finds its embryonic nucleus in the Church.

Gospel Reading

The Gospel reference to the fig tree gives us a word of hope. A fig tree, like most trees in winter, looks dead but in fact is bursting with new life ready to explode to the surface in the spring. The same is true of the Church and of our individual selves. Although we may be enduring difficulties, problems and apparent death, deep within us is the Holy Spirit from the day of our baptism. He is the nucleus of new life and rebirth. No matter what happens, we should not doubt the power of our call from God, our vocation, God's specific will for us. If we put our faith in the Lord's light, we can survive any darkness.

Point

Baptism reminds us that at the end of our spiritual winter, a bud will break through a crack in the concrete to start new life.

SATURDAY — Thirty-Fourth Week of the Year
Rv 22:1-7   Lk 21:34-36

First Reading

We come, at last, to the close of the Book of Revelation. It describes the nurturing water which flows from the throne of God. This is the river of spiritual life that gives vitality to people of all ages. From this rush of the Spirit of God, the great spiritual giants, martyrs and heroes of all ages are born. These are people who have received a life which death cannot destroy. They set their sight on a goal and on a Lord which are deathless. The Book of Revelation ends with an admonition to those suffering first Christians that the Lord is coming soon. He will come inevitably to each of us. We will recognize Him either as Comrade or Judge.

Gospel Reading

Jesus speaks about the suddenness of the end. The early Church expected an immediate parousia. The doctrine of the Lord's return has often been misinterpreted as a justification for non-involvement in efforts to care for the needy and to remedy social ills. This is not the position of the Church. We cannot sit with our hands folded waiting for Jesus to return to extirpate sin and wrongdoing. He also comes to us for an accounting. Our goal as individual Christians and as a Church is to prepare the way for the Lord's return. We are to turn people to the Lord, expose them to the life-giving sacramental waters and plant the seed of the Word deep into their hearts. The Church's role is not to pretend to be the new Jerusalem of God's final act of creation. Our purpose as a Church and a parish is to prepare people for whom and to whom the Lord will return. In every dark night, our role is to point to the coming morning.

Point

We are not called to simply await the Second Coming. We are called to prepare for it.

SPIRITUAL/PASTORAL and HOMILETIC RESOURCES FOR TODAY'S MINISTRY

THE PRIESTLY HEART
by: Most Rev. James A. Griffin
Written primarily to aid priests on their annual retreats, this work can be utilized by anyone who takes service to the Kingdom seriously. Bishop Griffin utilizes the scriptures, the mystics and writings of contemporary theologians in an invigorating manner that is guaranteed to refresh the heart of any priest and provide the depth and spiritual nourishment needed for our earthly pilgrimage with all of its opportunities and challenges.
149 pages   **$6.95, paper**

SPIRITUAL AIDS FOR THOSE IN RENEW
Ponderings, Poems and Promises
by: Bishop Robert F. Morneau
Bishop Morneau reflects in a delightful way on all the aspects of the RENEW program and its tremendous potential for bringing about a wholistic vitalization of our people, parishes and dioceses. These meditations can be used by laity and clergy alike as a basis for a better understanding of the RENEW program. The ponderings can be used as a stimulus for meditation for those not involved with the RENEW program but who are looking to deepen their union with God and others. The preacher and teacher will find innumerable insights applicable to a variety of speaking situations.
111 pages   **$4.50, paper**

SACRAMENTAL AND OCCASIONAL HOMILIES
by: Rev. David Q. Liptak
"Fr. Liptak offers some excellent examples of sermons to be used for various sacramental and liturgical purposes . . . a handy helper and idea-starter for the busy priest." *The Priest*
96 pages   **$4.95, paper**

These titles are availabe at your local BOOK STORE or from:
Alba House Publications
2187 Victory Blvd.
Staten Island, N.Y. 10314-6603